Dr. Kathrin Anne Meier

MASTERING CORPORATE LIFE

A Guide to Serenity and Success at Work

To Chris, thank you so much for all your good advice and insights. All the best and much happiness, sincerely,

Kathrin

RIVER GROVE
BOOKS

Published by River Grove Books
Austin, TX
www.rivergrovebooks.com

Distributed by River Grove Books

Design and composition by Greenleaf Book Group and Brian Phillips
Cover design by Greenleaf Book Group and Brian Phillips
Cover photo courtesy of Kammeran Gonzalez-Keola

Publisher's Cataloging-in-Publication data is available.

Print ISBN: 9781632996299

eBook ISBN: 9781632996305

First Edition

CONTENTS

INTRODUCTION

The best investment you can make is in yourself. Nobody can take away what you've got in yourself, and everybody has potential they haven't used yet.
—Warren Buffett

Let us first talk about *mastery*: Mastery is the achievement of a certain expert skill or knowledge. One can literally obtain a master's degree, such as a Master's in Business Administration, a Master of Science in Mathematics, or a Master's in Landscape Architecture. One can also become a Master Violin Maker, Master Goldsmith, or Master Farmer.

When you have mastered something, you will typically do it with ease, joy, and pride. And if you really like what you are doing, you additionally gain a sense of fulfillment. Achieving mastery is like jumping over a hurdle, though the process may take you longer. Good teachers and professors can help speed the process by explaining things well and comprehensibly in their courses or books and by assigning relevant exercises in the right sequence.

There are classes, training courses, tutorials, and schools for all kinds of subjects, not only to teach scientific or handcraft topics but also for the so-called "softer" skillset, which includes things such as social, interpersonal, and communication skills. In particular, in the business world, there is a growing body of management books that are meant to help you address specific aspects of work life, such as time management, skillful communication, networking, critical thinking, mindful work, etc. Typically, these books tend to be topic specific and based on research, and often, you have no choice but to read many pages in order to get the point. Hence, to get a holistic view, you need to do a lot of reading. However, it seems there is only little to be found in any of these genres on how to *holistically* master work life. This book aspires to fill this hole.

Now, let us talk about *corporate* life mastery and how we can have a work life that brings us ease, joy, and a sense of fulfillment. In corporations, work is divided among many people, and people's income often depends on the corporation's performance. Typically, goals are imposed on the employees by management with little room for self-determination on the overarching targets. Especially in large corporations, everyday work life can, at times, be tiring and frustrating, and can feel externally determined. Sometimes, people feel insignificant, just little cogs in a large machine. Sometimes, they set their hopes on career advancement, but cannot seem to move forward. They might aspire to reach the next step on the career ladder, but they are repeatedly overlooked for promotions.

Throughout my career, I saw many ambitious, well-educated people suffering because they worked extremely hard to advance their careers but still did not progress as they desired. Analyzing their situations, I often recognized similar patterns. Some people were striving to move up in the hierarchy without considering whether they would like the new type of work. In short, they were not clear about what they actually wanted. Others would concentrate so much on actually doing good work that they forgot to make their contributions known to a larger audience, and their managers were happy to not recognize them either in order to keep them in their current teams. Then there were people who were missing the sense and purpose in what they are doing, and so they started just doing the bare minimum. No wonder they did not feel fulfilled in their work life.

In all these cases, there was one common missing factor: *awareness*. Awareness of what really made their days joyful, what they truly wanted, and ultimately who they were.

Obtaining mastery in corporate work life in the context of this book means becoming an expert in self-awareness; it means mastering self-management as well as managing relationships with others.

But why would we really want to achieve mastery in the corporate world beyond the specific subjects we studied at university or elsewhere?

The answer is simple: Because we spend most of our days at work. People working for corporations often spend more time at work than they spend on healthy sleep, meals, and with their family or friends. Every day of the work week, people have less private time than work time. Hence, it makes sense that people should have a good time at work. But sadly, some people believe that work is only about earning money to make a living, and that there can be no other requirements for work, such as fun, joy, let alone fulfillment. They often focus on leisure time to feel alive and joyful. In my view, it is not wise to search for fulfillment only outside of work.

What is it anyway that humans are striving for in life? What is a good life? Many philosophers and spiritual leaders have written about these questions. One of the most concise answers comes from the Indian sage Maharishi Mahesh Yogi. He claims that the purpose of life is "the expansion of happiness and evolution is the process through which it is fulfilled." Whether in Western, Eastern, ancient, or more recent philosophies, one can find surprisingly similar statements of the meaning of life.

Happiness always involves positive emotions ranging from contentment and gratitude to pleasure and intense joy. Centuries ago, the Greek philosophers wrote about "hedonia" and "eudaimonia." A hedonic life is a *pleasant* life, full of pleasure and joy and free from pain. It is overall safe, calm, and serene. A eudemonic life is an *engaged* life, virtuous and purposeful, the individual flourishing. Additionally, modern psychologists studying happiness talk about "psychologically rich," *meaningful* lives, in which people experience a variety of positive and also negative emotions and therefore feel especially alive. Some people even claim their goal is not happiness or ease but the feeling of being alive, which one often finds in drama or exciting experiences. Which brings us back to the evolution part of the meaning of life. If humans only strove for happiness, we would probably still be sitting in trees eating ripe fruit, with no need to explore new worlds or invent new things. In fact, every development people have made can be interpreted as being in the direction of evolution and progress. And we strive for progress because achievement and reaching our goals along the way make us happy. It is like one of my favorite sayings about advancing in life: "If you are not growing, you are slowly dying." We naturally feel fulfilled when we are improving ourselves or our lives. Hence, we understand that life is about happiness in conjunction with evolution.

However happiness is defined, it seems deeply human to strive for a life full of joy, success, satisfaction, and fulfillment while unfolding evolutionary paths. My view is that evolution in the sense of development, change, and progress does not necessarily come from pain, suffering, or competition, as it is often described; it comes more from the joy of exploration and creation and the grand feeling of success we find in discovering new things. Success is the accomplishment of our aims, whereof the purest form is fulfillment.

Life mastery means being able to cope with whatever comes your way in a serene and composed manner. You apply your skills with great joy, peace, and inner happiness. Everything is seen as a learning experience. This does not mean that you will no longer experience adversity as such. Life will always have its ups and downs, and the low, dull moments you experience will only help you enjoy the wonderful moments of life even more. You simply have to make sure you do not stay in discomfort and let it ruin your life.

Life mastery also means raising self-awareness and self-confidence, knowing and getting what you want, having success, and living to your full potential. Having achievements and success by doing something you genuinely like and find meaningful is called fulfillment. In this spirit, corporate life mastery means achieving both a sense of purpose and fulfillment at work, as well as becoming more conscious about life in general.

Returning to the topic of life in corporate settings, although there is a large trend towards smaller, more agile company formations like boutiques or start-ups that often attract younger, exceptionally talented, innovative, energetic, and ambitious people, large corporations will remain relevant. Only the war for talent will increase, and corporations are well advised to make sure they can offer their employees fulfilling careers.

This book gives practical tips on how to overcome hurdles in the corporate world and how to deal with awkward encounters, such as jealousy, anger, arguments, and furtiveness in the work environment. It is about learning the skills you need to reach agreements with others, find "best" solutions, make yourself heard, and ultimately shape your life according to your own wishes and beliefs. It will bring happiness, flow, fulfillment and meaning, as well as serenity and a sense of effortlessness into your life. In addition, as a nice side effect, it will raise your mental health, satisfaction, and productivity as well. When you have achieved life mastery, everything—literally everything—will give you more joy, happiness, inner peace, and contentment.

Having gone through this process myself and with many employees and mentees, I feel compelled to describe my insights in this book.

The first chapter describes some basic mindset skills and concepts such as thinking and believing. It explains how your beliefs shape your reality and how they can be changed to improve your whole life in a profound way. The second chapter explains the importance of knowing what you really want and how you can discover purpose in your life. The content of these first two chapters is not necessarily specific to corporate work life but provides an important foundation for the topics that follow. The next chapter explains specific aspects of self-management, including how to effectively formulate goals and milestones and how to organize your time and energy. It also describes how to position yourself, how you can develop yourself, and how you can gain more self-confidence overall. The fourth chapter is about managing your relationships and offers tips on effective networking and guidance on how to advance your career in the direction you desire, as well as how you can make yourself visible and heard by those who decide your promotion and advancement. The last chapter gives advice to managers who want to implement the themes of this book with their team or the people they lead. It describes the need for diversity and inclusion and provides guidance on how to support individual employees or entire teams.

From your own education you know that mastery takes time, energy, persistence, and determination. The only thing you need for this book is the determination to engage with the topic—the rest is made easy for you. Once you have read and realized the basic concepts herein, you will want to apply them immediately. A good, meaningful life is its own motivation.

HOW TO USE THIS BOOK

You are what you do, not what you say you will do.

—Carl Gustav Jung

This book is based on my own experience of a long and successful corporate career. It contains many insights I gained through my work, particularly through working with my teams and numerous mentees, as well as through much reading and thinking about related topics. In this book, each topic is described and complemented with real-life examples from my corporate experience. They are marked with grey frames. I have also included effective, practical exercises to go along with each lesson.

In my career, I worked in a number of very different settings. Although the companies I worked for were always part of large corporations, I have worked in both smaller and larger organizational settings. Hence, I gained experience in boutique-style and much bigger organizations, all of them in a global environment. Also, I worked as a top specialist and served in various leadership and board functions. Additionally, through my extensive network as well as through public speaking at conferences, I gained many insights from other fields and industries.

Especially through working with my mentees and the mentoring programs I organized, I often saw struggle, pain, and unfulfilled career wishes. I also realized how much knowledge of basic life principles many people are missing. Through studying the problems of my mentees and helping them overcome them, I gained many insights regarding career development in corporates. Though, most importantly, I saw how little it took to do something about the adverse situations, to enhance them and permanently change people's lives for the better. Each time, I was astonished and delighted to see how people flourished and got what they wanted with only the slightest change. You could really see them beginning to master their corporate lives.

Therefore, I decided to write this book in order to teach a broader audience what I taught to my mentees. I also added some thoughts for managers who might want to create a work environment where people can flourish and progress and bring their best to work.

Although the chapters and sections of this book build on each other, it might be that you are already familiar with some of the content. If that is the case, feel free to skip those sections. I have intentionally gone into detail on many topics to meet the needs of readers who may have varying levels of familiarity with those topics. However, for any content you are encountering for the first time, you can get the most out of this book by doing the exercises that follow each section. Learning is so much more effective when you can relate what you have read to your environment and directly apply the knowledge you gained. I recommend getting a notebook in which you can write the results or outcomes of the exercises. In this way, you will easily make progress and become aware of your progress and growth.

Most likely, you will need several days or even weeks to digest and work through the book completely, as some exercises require time for observation and reflection.

This book is not only to read, but is also designed to be interactive. Always remember that you will make progress only by doing. There is no way to advance simply by reading and understanding. You must implement new knowledge and skills to get real transformation. Applying the concepts of the book will bring you phenomenal success, and the achievement of working through this book will expand your happiness.

I wish you a great time on your journey to mastering your corporate life.

Chapter 1

YOUR INNER WORLD

On thoughts

Our life is what our thoughts make it.

— Marcus Aurelius

The day I truly realized that we are 100 percent responsible for our lives, my life completely changed. In one instant, jealousy was fully gone. Comparing myself to others, worrying that they can do something better, or that their ideas are superior to mine—all this was wiped away. I also realized that complaining about something or someone is totally unnecessary. How did this happen?

At that time, about twenty-five years ago, I was studying the universal laws of life in a book called *The Seven Spiritual Laws of Success* by the Indian American medical doctor and spiritual leader Deepak Chopra (1994). That was more or less the first time I read about how thoughts shape our complete lives. Of course, I might have read about the power of thoughts before, but I obviously had not fully realized it. Everyone understands that thoughts are at the beginning of creating anything new, whether it is a new house, a new book, a new concept, a new process, or any other brand of novelty. However, most people are not aware that negative thoughts bring us negative outcomes and, conversely, that positive thoughts bring us positive outcomes.

Being 100 percent responsible for my life means being 100 percent responsible for my thoughts. It is my thoughts that determine how I cope with a specific circumstance, another person, or another matter. And it is my thoughts that make me take action. Always remember: you are responsible for your own thoughts, and only you can change them. By understanding that your life is what your thoughts make it, you will want to change your thoughts towards those that bring you happiness and joy.

Twenty-five years ago, I came to this sudden understanding that my thoughts shape my day and ultimately my entire life. My thoughts stand at the beginning of whatever I want to achieve, and my thoughts bring forward that achievement. With that, I understood that I am on my own distinct path and everyone else is on his or her distinct path, and thus envying others does not make any sense. If someone has something nicer, can do something better, responds in a better way than I, then the best reaction is to enjoy this and potentially ask myself whether I really desire to have that characteristic, skill, or object too. Then, I think about what steps I need to take to get what I desire.

If you really desire to have a specific characteristic, surround yourself with people showing this characteristic, or read books about people with this characteristic. Try to learn from them, but do not envy them, as this is not useful. It will only bring you into an inactive and stagnant role of a victim who cannot change a situation. In the corporate context, this means that if you meet someone in your company who has a trait you admire, you should try to work together on something or get the person to mentor you. We will see how to best do that later in this book.

In the next section, we will see that we often wish for things we already have a predisposition for, and that we will generally not have true wishes that are totally out of our reach. Our dreams may be a long way off, but they are not impossible to fulfill. Typically, at forty years old, we will not wish deeply from our hearts to be twenty again. We know that to be impossible. Instead, we might wish to be as independent and blameless as we were back then. Then we can reason how we could get some of that independence back in our lives. Maybe you have responsibilities that prevent you from getting full independence. You can decide how far you want to go to become more independent and decide on next steps.

The question is, how can we be sure about these insights? Is it really only our thoughts that make our lives? And is it really happiness through evolution that we strive for? How can we know? There are two answers to this question.

First, this knowledge has been around since ancient times. Greeks and Romans wrote about it, and in every century, you can find philosophers and other scholars who felt the same way. This knowledge was recorded and referred to as "universal laws," or natural, spiritual, or mental laws. These are the very basic laws of life. They are so generic and so fundamental that no intelligent being really can argue against them.

Second, there is more and more current research on these topics. At leading universities, for example, significant work is being done around mindset, social, and positive psychology. To name just a few publications: *Mindset* by Carol S. Dweck (2006), *The Happiness Advantage* by Shawn Achor (2010), *Flourish* and *Learned Optimism* by Martin E.P. Seligman (2011, 1990), and *Happier* by Tal Ben-Shahar (2007). In essence, these researchers describe and prove these universal laws in scientific terms.

In this book, I will not necessarily cite the newest studies, as these fields are constantly advancing, but I will present some universal laws of life that really make a difference if you apply them in your own daily existence. Typically, living according to the universal laws of life brings ease and effortlessness as well as deeper understanding and meaning into your life. Most universal laws are somehow related. However, for the purpose of understanding the concepts in this book, it is sufficient to concentrate on a few.

What I also like about the universal laws is that they are principle-based and not rule-based. You must always remember rules, and there can be a confusingly large number of them. Principles only need to be understood one time, and then applying them follows naturally.

More and more schools are starting to teach these topics, and I am convinced that in the not-too-distant future, knowledge around the universal laws, or the respective academic findings, will be a standard subject in schools. Some universities, and also corporations, have already introduced or started to discuss the subject under the name of happiness, mindfulness, applied philosophy, or similar.

What we have heard thus far is an important aspect of the universal "law of pure potentiality." It means that everything has the potential to become realized if it is in line with our own nature and evolution. The "law of attraction," one of the most powerful universal laws, also comes into play. That law states that we draw into our lives everything that is alive in us—everything we think, believe, and feel—whether consciously or subconsciously. The basis of the "law of attraction" is that thoughts create matter. Now, if everything starts with a thought, we might as well start to have constructive and helpful thoughts.

Negative thinking

Too often, I see people with a tendency to think negatively. They speak negatively about their managers, their coworkers, their projects, and even worse, about themselves and their lives. In fact, research shows that of an average person's approximately 70,000 thoughts per day, a very large amount of those are negative (Seligman 2011). With so much negativity, it becomes difficult to live a content and joyful life. When asked about any negative thoughts they might harbor, people typically respond that no one can see their thoughts and so they believe it is enough if they act kindly to the outside world. However, thinking negatively while acting positively uses up much of their energy, and they will most probably finish with worse outcomes than if they thought positively to begin with. At least, their own happiness would be considerably elevated if they would start thinking more positive thoughts. Research shows that people who think positively, rather than negatively, are higher achievers and have better overall health. They are less likely to give up in the face of adversity and suffer less from depression.

The question is, why do we have negative thoughts anyway? Is the mind trying to make sense of the world? Some people say that our focus on negative things actually comes from our ancestors and again from their ancestors and so on. For example, when we lie in bed having undetermined fear, or fears about our future, we are most probably living through a pattern we have learned from our parents, which was implicitly taught to them by our grandparents, and so on into prehistory. This all goes back to the time when our ancestors had to physically fear for their lives because they were not safe at night and needed to be alert all the time. Those who were more attuned to the danger and more aware of the bad things lurking around them were more likely to survive. However, these days, most of us do not have to physically fear for our lives when lying in bed. Hence, we may as well decide not to be afraid in that moment and instead think of something positive before going to sleep. Once you have understood this, you are able to stop fearing for yourself at night—and almost more importantly, not pass it on to further generations. And just like that, you will feel much better.

Regardless of why we have specific negative thoughts in particular moments, the strategy for avoiding all unnecessary negative thoughts is actually the same: Try to dismiss the negative thought and think a positive one instead. Sometimes, a bit more is needed to send a bad thought away; try, for instance, to say something like "not today" or "not now." You can almost always find a positive thought in any given situation.

Thinking negatively can have a devastating impact on our lives. Often, negative thinking leads to repeated negative thinking, and then a negative spiral begins. This builds up anger and not only results in a bad mood, but also builds up stress and can even spiral into a depression. If you do not stop the spiral, it may have a serious impact on your health. Equally bad, it brings down your self-confidence considerably.

Hence, at first, the most important step is to *become aware* of your thoughts, then to improve the quality of your thoughts. This will lead to remarkable improvements in the area of life to which you apply it.

As an example, you might have had a great day, but then a colleague makes a negative comment about your work. You might then let his words stew inside your head for the rest of the working day. In the evening, when asked, you might say you had a terrible day, although it was actually good overall despite that one negative incident. Life mastery means to become aware of your thoughts and reflect with compassion on whether this person has a genuine critique about your quality of work or whether he was just looking for an outlet for his own dissatisfaction. Then you can freely choose your reaction. You can calmly decide whether you would like to change something about your work product or not. In the end, if you stay strong and positive, you will have a much better outcome for your whole day.

Please do not confuse avoiding negative thinking with avoiding negative feelings. It is important to acknowledge and accept negative feelings fully. It is normal for us humans to be afraid, feel pain, or mourn. However, it does not make sense to constantly come back to the same negative feelings. You should take the opportunity to look closer and think about how you can process the feelings and let them go as soon as possible.

When negative thinking comes along with strong negative feelings, for instance when you get upset by someone else's actions or behavior, Martin E.P. Seligman suggests in his book *Learned Optimism* (1990) that you consciously challenge the negative thinking by first noting your reaction and what made you feel negatively. Then at a later stage, once you have calmed down, reflect on whether you could have interpreted the situation differently with more understanding for the party or matter causing your negative feelings, and think about how you could have reacted alternatively. Over time, realizing that your thoughts could also be more hopeful and positive will turn your thinking and feeling towards more positivity and optimism. Seligman empirically showed that everyone can learn optimism and that doing so can not only prevent depression, but also help you achieve more and improve your physical health.

OVERCOMING NEGATIVITY: EXAMPLE FROM THE CORPORATE WORLD

I worked from time to time with a woman who was consistently negative. She spoke negatively about her supervisor, her colleagues, the work products of others, and the company as a whole. She often got upset about situations that objectively were not worth getting upset about. It was obvious that she did not know any better and had probably learned this pattern of reaction from her early childhood environment. Unfortunately, even though she was exceptionally well trained, she was not promoted after a certain period of time and was unhappy about it. Her consistent bad mood severely limited her ability to develop. She was literally trapped because she was so easily upset. Instead, one reaction at a time, she should have reflected on why she was having a negative emotion and what exactly was behind her getting upset about a certain situation. Then she could have put that one thing behind her, and next time, she would either not have had to get upset at all or would have gotten out of her bad mood very quickly. However, she should not pass over her feelings or simply put them away, as this can create inner pressure that may result in physical illnesses over time. Likewise, she could have become aware of her negative thoughts and replaced them with positive ones. This would have made her a person that everyone would enjoy working with and someone management would want to promote.

Choosing your thoughts

Knowing that your thoughts form your reality and your outcomes, first thing in the morning, you should start your days with positive thoughts, independent of the mood you wake up with. Just becoming aware of negative thinking, meaning catching negative thoughts and then thinking something positive, will change the situation and will shape your day for the better.

What about those who feel they have a miserable life, and can find nothing positive to say in this moment? The trick is to say something positive anyway. Anything true will do: "Luckily, I am alive"; "The sun is beautifully shining"; "I am grateful for my children"; "My day will be better than yesterday"; or even, "I will have a wonderful day." With that, something will change, as the human mind works that way.

In the past, many people have wondered and derided this technique as ineffective and stupid, talking about toxic positivity. Most certainly, they applied it in an unfavorable way. Whatever honest, largely attainable, and positive thing you say to yourself will be picked up by your subconscious mind. This is the reason why you will unconsciously behave differently afterwards. It will influence your decisions, large and small.

Being aware of our thoughts and changing them to be more positive, sometimes even against the current state we are in, is an important part to mastering our life.

Before every important meeting, and especially before potentially difficult meetings, I think positively about the meeting by saying to myself things like: "This is a good meeting. We make optimal decisions for the company's best outcome. Participants cooperate and contribute meaningfully." Despite my apprehensions, none of these meetings in fact turned out to be unfriendly, tenacious, or painful. On the contrary, they turned out to be concentrated, constructive, and effective.

POSITIVELY INFLUENCING DIFFICULT MEETINGS

I still vividly remember a potentially difficult meeting with our regulators. Many of my colleagues were really nervous about what time-consuming things they might require from us. Word had gotten around before the meeting that the regulators were in particularly bad moods that day. Since I had to chair the meeting, it was up to me to lighten their better mood. I had mentally prepared exactly as described above and the regulators began the meeting already in a positive and above all cooperative mood. It was a meeting where everyone took their place and position, and there was a lot of mutual understanding and trust. Much to the astonishment of my colleagues, we also did not get any unreasonable findings and more unnecessary, tedious tasks to complete.

LOOKING AHEAD

Another time, while on a business trip, I had to meet someone who was known for being moody and troublesome. I had a difficult subject to discuss, which I was sure he would not like. Immediately before the meeting

I prepared as just described, and to my own amazement the meeting went very well. My message, though not enthusiastically received, did not result in an outburst of anger or dissatisfaction, and all my requests were successfully met. On the other hand, I remember another meeting for which I had not prepared myself mentally, and which went so badly that none of my requests were accepted. Since then, I never forget to prepare myself mentally before a difficult meeting.

Similar thinking can be used to smooth the way for work projects. If you believe your project will be cumbersome and unsatisfying, and will potentially never be finished, chances are high that this will be the case. You might encounter difficulties and probably many stressful moments. However, independent of what your first thoughts are about your project, if you think optimistically about your project, chances are not only much higher that it comes to a good end, but that it will also be more joyful to work on the project and you will be more satisfied with the outcome. Typically, I start a project thinking: "This project is important and brings my company forward. Those of us working on it will have great fun and enjoy the process. It will have a great outcome, it serves the company well, and management is grateful for our work." At a later stage, when a project is running and challenges arise, as they typically do in any meaningful project, I repeat these sentences and add potentially new, even more powerful ones.

Obviously, the more conscious you are of your thoughts, the more purposeful and powerful they become.

Knowing all this, we appreciate that thinking positively will bring good things to our lives. However, from time to time, you also hear voices against it. These people say it is part of a fulfilled life to get upset, find others impossible, or make other people jealous. They consider it salt in the soup. I understand that a little bit of drama in life can, for instance, make project work more fun. It energizes people. However, constant drama is not helpful for making progress, whether on a project or related to other matters, and definitely is not good for your own health. *Better to enjoy your little bit of drama, if you want to, and then consciously step out of it and move on.* It makes an enormous difference if you can choose the level of drama you want in your life but not be at the mercy of it. Being able to control your thoughts and mind is an important part of life mastery.

Summary

- Universal laws are very basic principles that describe life. They have been known since ancient times. These days, serious research is done around the topics they describe.

- Our thoughts are decisive of our lives.

- Positive thoughts will bring positive outcomes. Negative thoughts will bring negative outcomes.

- The first step is becoming conscious of our thoughts. The second is taking responsibility for them in our heads.

- We should choose our thoughts consciously because the thoughts that appear in our heads will take on their respective forms in the outside world.

Exercises

1. Do you have a situation that is not going well for you at work? For instance, a disagreement with a coworker, a misalignment with your manager, a project that is not running well? Write down a few thoughts you have about your particular circumstance. Are they positive or negative? In case the thoughts are negative, formulate a few thoughts you could have about the relationship or situation that are positive and constructive. Independent of the situation, write down how you would ideally like things to be. Most probably, you will notice the situation change soon after doing this.

2. Observe your thoughts for one full day. Whenever a negative thought arises, take note of it and search for a positive replacement instead. In the evening, reflect on these instances.

3. Do this at least once: In the morning, write down what you have on your agenda or how the schedule of your day will most probably look. You can build your day in sections (i.e., breakfast, first meeting, telephone call, second meeting, time to check email, lunch, and so forth). For each section, write down your immediate first thought about it. In case it is negative or neutral, write down something positive next to it. Throughout the day, remember the positive statements before each section of your day begins. In the evening, go through the list and reflect on how these positive thoughts influenced the outcome of your work and encounters that day. I am sure you will have positive insights. Plus, if you do this daily, your life will surely change for the better.

Change from within

Respect yourself and others will respect you.

—Confucius

For the development of your own consciousness, one of the most important universal laws is the "law of correspondence." It says that patterns repeat throughout our lives and within other lives and living beings around us. Aspects of it are also known as the "law of mirrors," which states that whatever you see in other people is a reflection of what you have inside of yourself.

Let me give you an example: Say you encountered something annoying that puts you in a particularly bad mood, and even worse, you might then interact with someone who gets in a bad mood too because of you. It is contagious. Once in a while, you will find individuals who do not mirror other people's bad moods. They just stay calm and serene. The bad mood, or more precisely whatever caused it, does not resonate within them.

This is equally true for others' attitudes and views that disturb us. We carry those views within ourselves as well—otherwise they would not disturb us.

Now, if the outside is a reflection of our inside, then whatever we want to see differently in our outside world, we can begin to change from within. And we may realize that only we ourselves can change. This means we do not necessarily need to change our partner, manager, or home location. All we have to do is change ourselves, because if we change, everything will change for us.

It starts with changing how we react in situations that typically provoke negative emotions in us. We can choose not to get angry, not to regret, not to feel guilt, not to become jealous. We ourselves are fully responsible in how we handle these situations. If someone is aggressive towards you, you can choose to reply calmly, let the person know that you understand why he or she is upset, and communicate how you feel about the matter. Then you can calmly address what you would like the other person to do differently. If you think it through, you are responsible for almost all situations you are in and you are always responsible for how you handle these situations.

In the corporate world, I regularly have people complain to me that individuals lack respect. This can be a lack of respect for a person, or for a person's work or achievements. The same thing applies here: It is likely that these individuals lack respect for themselves. Most of the time, it is not an obvious lack of respect, but something much more subtle. It has to do with lacking full self-acceptance, where they accept themselves with all their faults and strengths.

Signs of low self-respect and/or low self-esteem include needing constant validation from the outside. Someone lacking self-esteem might make a fool of themselves at a party or in the office, or let others control them such that they no longer rule their own lives. They often say yes to things others want them to do, but they actually do not want to do them. They also tend to take on far more work than they can reasonably handle, which may land them in difficult situations. Typically, we are our own worst critics by thinking that everything we do is not good enough, that *we* are not good enough. This also may lead us to judge others. The more a person does this, the more he or she lacks self-respect. Another sign of low self-esteem is when people behave arrogantly or dismissively towards others. They typically need to belittle someone else in order to feel good about themselves.

In any case, lacking self-respect can considerably lower the quality of your life and can even lead to depression. Self-respect is crucial for happiness. It is also the foundation of strong and healthy relationships with other people.

High self-respect goes along with the courage to stand by your values and beliefs. You do not need constant comparison with others, as you feel good about your attributes, talents, and abilities. You can openly share your passions and opinions. You stay honest, you speak up, and you can communicate how you really feel. You understand your limits and can say no if something is beyond them. You respect your needs first before you try to meet someone else's. In summary, people with high self-respect fully accept themselves as they are.

There is another universal law that comes into play here, which is the "law of giving and receiving." This law is similar to the "law of mirrors," but while the latter is more static or instant, this law addresses the dynamic. It says that you have to give what you want to get. This is obvious for love and especially true for success. If you want to get appreciation, give appreciation. If you create happiness for others, you create happiness for yourself.

As Deepak Chopra nicely explains in his book *The Seven Spiritual Laws of Success* (1994), "Practicing the 'law of giving and receiving' is actually very simple: if you want joy, give joy to others; if you want love, learn to give love; if you want attention and appreciation, learn to give attention and appreciation; if you want material affluence, help others to become materially affluent. In fact, the easiest way to get what you want is to help others get what they want."

It is impossible to demand that you be loved. Only by giving love can you, often instantly, receive love back. It is like a circle. What you give, you will receive.

Most importantly, when you give, it needs to be genuine. You must give with joy. Reluctance in giving does not provide the same effect. And the more you give wholeheartedly and unconditionally, the more you will get.

EXAMPLES ON CORRESPONDENCE

I have always taught my team: "If you want to be successful, you have to give success." This is especially true in one's relationship with a direct supervisor. Too often in corporations, I saw people trying to outdo their supervisors because they thought they could do their supervisor's work better themselves. These individuals obviously did not fully respect their supervisors and took every opportunity to show that they are smarter than their boss, for example, showing off in meetings with or without the supervisor present. Most people in these meetings see through this unpleasant behavior immediately. Of course, the supervisor also notices this and will make sure that the employee does not become too strong, for instance by withholding important information. If, on the contrary, the employee had made the supervisor successful by sharing successes or giving credit even in front of others, the supervisor would have behaved exactly the opposite way, doing everything possible to help the employee succeed. And when time came for a new job, the supervisor would make sure the employee made a good career move by opening opportunities or giving excellent references.

There are so many examples I could give to illustrate the point about the inner and outer world. A prominent one is the way customers are treated. If you believe that a customer is trying to hide something from you, for example, to get a better price, your suspicion is often based on the fact that you are trying to hide something as well, or you are neutral at best towards your customer. If, on the other hand, you try to help your customer succeed by providing them with exactly what they need, or if you do everything you can to help your customer succeed—without putting yourself unduly at risk, of course—your customer will be more than willing to pay the fair price and stay loyal to you for a long time.

STOP COMPLAINING

Another example from my corporate life: Years ago, it felt like my office was full of people complaining all the time. Everyone who came in complained about something, be it an overly demanding client, their unfair manager, or just stress in general. And I listened and confirmed to them that life is at times annoying and unfair. It began to annoy me that seemingly everyone came into my office to complain, but I did not know what to do about it. As I began to study the universal laws of life, I realized that I too was a person who complained all the time. I did not necessarily always complain to others, but mostly to myself. So I did the most important thing and stopped complaining to myself. What a relief when I stopped doing that! Soon after, almost no one came anymore to my office to complain. They just did not have the sounding board for it anymore.

Following these universal laws, you will realize that the individuals around us become our teachers. It requires some courage and honesty to look into the mirror and acknowledge what you see. However, facing yourself will bring you deep insights and will strengthen your personality. It will put an end to you feeling like a victim, and you will blame others or circumstances less and less. It will let you take responsibility for yourself.

After all, please remember, unfriendliness can only bring more unfriendliness, disrespect only disrespect, and hate only hate. And kindness, light, and joy, in turn, can spring only from positive thought—never otherwise.

Having heard all this, it becomes obvious that doing something for others gives us great happiness and satisfaction. Whenever you must make a choice, for instance on how to further develop your career or where to put your efforts, this is a good thought to keep in mind. This topic has been extensively researched by Adam Grant and described in his book *Give and Take: Why Helping Others Drives Our Success* (2014).

I would like to close this section by a quote I believe is from Deepak Chopra: "You can only give what you have, and your relationships will always mirror how you feel about yourself. Are you treating yourself as the precious lovable soul you are? Infinitely worthy? Infinitely subserving? In the words of the Buddha: You can search the entire universe and not find a single being more worthy of love than you."

Summary

- Our outer world is a reflection of our inner world.

- "We discover ourselves through others." —Carl Gustav Jung

- If a person does not give us due respect, we may want to explore whether we respect ourselves enough.

- We cannot change others, but we ourselves can change.

- What you want to receive, you have to give. Make sure you give unconditionally and wholeheartedly.

Exercises

1. Think of a person you find unsympathetic. Try to determine which characteristic you dislike in this person. Explore what aspect of this characteristic you dislike in yourself. (Note, sometimes it takes me two days to figure out what it might be!) If you like, you can then think about what you could do differently to change this characteristic in yourself, for instance, reacting in another way the next time you would otherwise show this characteristic. Do this just for yourself, independent of the person you found unsympathetic.

2. Think about your best friends. What characteristics of theirs do you like most? More than likely, they will share some common characteristics. You can be proud, too, because chances are high that you have those same characteristics yourself. Most of the time, we are not aware of this, though.

3. Think about a situation where you did not get the respect you wanted. Think back to whether you respected the other person beforehand. Reflect on whether you have enough self-respect, or whether you sometimes think badly about yourself, or whether you treat yourself badly at times. Think about how you could better respect yourself.

4. For one entire day, pay attention to how often you say something disrespectful to yourself, like "I am too stupid" if something did not work out, or "I never will get this" when you do not understand something at first. These sentences diminish you and block your progress. You would not allow anyone else to talk to you like this, so why say these things to yourself? In the evening, reflect on how often you used disrespectful thinking towards yourself and make a promise to yourself to get rid of these thoughts immediately.

5. An exercise for the more advanced: Before your next meeting, silently think of something good about each person and silently give them a gift, something like joy, fun, luck, or happiness. Reflect after the meeting, and when you meet these people the next time, observe whether something has changed.

On beliefs

Whether you think you can, or you think you can't—you're right.

—Henry Ford

Our beliefs are our convictions about something. We may hold them consciously or unconsciously; however, they determine our lives. Some strengthen us, some weaken us, and some even limit us. Some are old—from our childhood, from our parents, teachers, or schoolmates—and some are newer—from work colleagues, managers, our partner, or social media. They can even come from books we read or movies we watch. They can be individual or collective beliefs.

For example, a person may have had someone tell him that he is not talented in sports. He may have even said that about himself when he was not performing at his best. Therefore, the person believed he was not talented, lost interest in sports, and was unable to develop further skills in that area. Now consider if instead he had heard words of support telling him he excelled in sports. The result would most likely have been different. Of course, you cannot make an Olympic champion out of an unathletic person, but the person can at least still enjoy sports.

Collective beliefs can be a difficult topic, because they are extremely tough to get rid of even if they are incorrect. Certain beliefs might be held in one part of the world, but in another, the problem does not exist, or people at least do not behave according to the same beliefs. As an example, one of the most mistaken collective beliefs widely held in Europe and North America is that the mathematical talent of women is inferior to that of men. This idea is so prevalent that from a young age, you can find differences in common interests and average math performances between girls and boys. However, there are countries where no such difference exists. Extensive studies have investigated this, and no clear answer has been found yet. However, meta studies describe the cause of this phenomenon as a mixture of socio-cultural factors, education, and environment—all external influences.

Our world is a reflection of our beliefs, and our actions are largely determined by our beliefs, i.e., the convictions we hold. Often concrete results or successes do not come about because someone has done particularly well or was particularly clever. Success is to be found in the fact that those people have the right convictions about themselves.

We do not know all our convictions, but all of us carry many negative ones with us. We have adopted them mostly unconsciously, starting already from early childhood, but have also continually collected them throughout our lives. Most of the time, negative thought patterns are destructive and can massively disturb our peace of mind. The study of them is of particular interest to many, because we can do something about the ones we wish to get rid of: We can decide to give them up and replace them with something that strengthens and supports us.

However, we need to be careful of how we do that. Because the unconscious mind works with images and words, we immediately understand that we cannot just negate a belief. We need to find an opposite image, so to speak, to replace the false belief. In the example from above, this could be envisioning yourself winning in your favorite sport, combined with a sentence like: "I am capable of learning a sport" or simply, "I am good at sports."

Obviously, the more often we reinforce our new beliefs, the stronger they will become.

MAKING YOUR MIND UP TO SUCCEED

Recently, I met someone who performed poorly in primary and secondary school, and his teachers openly told him that at the age of sixteen he was already a failure and would not achieve anything in his life. Years later, he proved them wrong and became a successful general manager of an exclusive hotel after having worked extremely hard, almost to exhaustion. Obviously, he did not believe his teachers, because he made it to the top in spite of what they said. However, their words, unconsciously present in his mind, made him work almost beyond his limits. If he had had supportive teachers around him, he surely could have become as successful without so much pain.

TEAM RESULTS BEYOND EXPECTATIONS

Another example from the corporate world comes from working with a team. When I hear managers speaking negatively about their teams, I always tell them, "If you believe your team is lazy, stupid, and unmotivated, your team will most likely be lazy, stupid, and unmotivated. If, however, you think highly of your team, they will produce outcomes you never would have imagined."

> This is true for whole teams, but also for each individual team member as such. Generally, my teams have achieved extraordinary things, and I have seen so many of my employees deliver results beyond what they themselves would have thought possible.

There is also modern research on reinforcement. One study shows that if people, before taking an IQ test, read that IQ is changeable instead of being genetically fixed, their IQ scores improved from earlier test data. Put another way, believing change is possible makes change possible (Dweck 2006).

Knowing this gives you a lot of power. Just remember, you can stop negative, aggressive, and limiting thoughts by, first, becoming aware of them and, second, by replacing them with something positive that is supporting you. In the next section, I will present you with a tool for how to do that effectively. Everyone can rise above his or her limitations. By updating your belief system, you can become a better version of yourself. If you get out of your own way and start believing in yourself, you can achieve great things.

Summary

- Beliefs are convictions that we often unconsciously adopt from other people.

- Our belief system is constantly in process, starting in early childhood and continuing until now.

- We can actively change our beliefs to positive ones, laying the groundwork for success.

Exercises

1. More than likely, you have negative beliefs about yourself that hold you back in areas like your private life, your professional life, your finances, or your health. Write them all down. Think about where these beliefs come from (however, you do not need to analyze them in great depth). Select from this list those beliefs you want to get rid of. Cross them out and replace them with a more supporting belief, using positive, powerful wording. Think about them regularly, at least daily, over a period of time. Exploring this topic and changing your beliefs could take a while, but it will certainly be beneficial to you.

2. Keep a list of your new beliefs in your notes. Enjoy reading them several times a day until you internalize them.

The power of affirmations and visualizations

Whatever we plant in our subconscious mind and nourish with repetition and emotion will one day become a reality.

—Earl Nightingale

Affirmations and visualizations are one of the fastest and most straightforward methods to positively program our subconscious mind and to sustainably change wrong patterns or negative beliefs, to build new habits, or to achieve our goals. Affirmations are short, positive statements that specify a certain situation, a habit, or a goal we want to gain or achieve. Visualizations are the corresponding image or visual process of the affirmation. In order to make them effective, affirmations and visualizations need to be frequently repeated, either aloud or silently in your mind.

Affirmations are much more than positive thinking, as they also reach and train the subconscious mind. Your conscious mind can choose what it accepts or rejects. However, your subconscious mind just accepts what you feel and believe to be true. Hence, the more you feel what you want, the better.

Particularly, you should reinforce your positive affirmations and visualizations just before sleeping. Never fall asleep in fear or doubt. Best is to fall asleep with a feeling of gratitude or success.

Likewise, a good time to repeat your affirmations and visualizations is when you wake up, even before you get out of bed. If you have several affirmations, it can be useful to write them down and read them first thing in the morning. You will be able to observe how much better your day will be.

Another ideal time to repeat your affirmations and do your visualizations is when you are already feeling good. If you are in doubt, or you have the feeling that you are missing something, let it be. In those moments, it will not work and is rather counterproductive.

Hence, if you would like to overcome limiting beliefs or if you would like to get rid of recurring negative thoughts, come up with a brief positive sentence, formulated in present tense, best accompanied by an image, and repeatedly think of it. When affirmation and visualization are combined, the effect is extraordinarily strong. In addition, the more you become excited about what you would like to have or become, the faster and easier you will achieve it.

As an example, a good affirmation for raising self-esteem is "I am good enough," or even better "I am enough." These simple statements have so much power.

Other examples of affirmations are:

- If you wish to be more patient:
  "My patience span is increasing every day."

- If you would like to have more friends:
  "I have good friends. They enjoy my company."

- If you lack pleasant moments:
  "My life is full of happiness and joy."

- If you are too quick-tempered:
  "I am calm and relaxed in every situation."

- If you have a doubt about an outcome:
  "I am successful in whatever I do."

- If you are struggling with yourself:
  "I am at peace with myself and with the world."

- If you are facing an unpleasant family situation that cannot be easily resolved: "There is great love in our family."

You may think this is not working, as the affirmations you are repeating to yourself are not true yet. However, starting with these sentences will change something in your life. In the last example, you might think that there is no great love in your family because you have frequent disputes with family members. However, if you start with this affirmation and if you feel love towards your family, you will see changes despite the unpleasant situation you are in at the moment. It will probably start with small signs, such as some smiles or understanding. Just observe how the situation unfolds and be grateful for any sign of improvement.

Results can come at a different pace. It could be that they appear immediately, in a few hours, a few days, or a few weeks. Frequent repetition is the key. Sometimes it takes saying it to yourself many hundreds of times, but it does help and actually makes all the difference. To let go of an old belief and replace it with a new and better one typically can take between ten days and three weeks. It depends on your focus and the situation and on how strongly you believe and feel it. Hence the process takes head and heart. There is no means to strive for something you find totally unrealistic. Also, whatever you wish for needs to be to the highest good of everything and everyone. In any case, be grateful for every sign of improvement.

It goes without saying that the affirmations need to be empowering and positively phrased. Negative affirmations, those that are not constructive, are also called negative self-talk. Negative self-talk increases difficulties and problems because you are focusing on the problems and not on the solutions. Negative feelings will follow, which are particularly potent, as we just learned. Just be aware that where you put your thoughts, your energy will flow, and that this is true whether you think positively or negatively. And whatever you practice is what will grow stronger. In any case, it is wiser to spend your time and energy thinking about solutions, improvements, and progress than about problems, deterioration, regression, and loss. In addition, the more your affirmations and visualizations make you move forward, the more you will achieve and the more you will feel good, happy, and motivated to continue in this positive direction.

In my view, there is nothing more important to realize than the fact that our thoughts form our lives. Whatever we repeat, whether it is good or bad, we can instill in our brains. We can be trapped repeating negative or unhelpful thoughts, such as critical self-talk, that will make our lives miserable. Or we can repeat positive things that are in our favor and will lighten up our lives. With that, I am sure you understand how important it is to think good thoughts about yourself. You do not necessarily need to put yourself on a pedestal, but you need to be kind to yourself and appreciate your being with all your talents and gifts.

Summary

- Affirmations are short positive statements which specify a certain situation, a habit, or a goal we want to gain or achieve, and visualizations are the corresponding image or visual process.

- Frequently repeating affirmations and visualizations can be a powerful tool for changing wrong patterns or negative beliefs, building new habits, or achieving goals.

- Affirmations in combination with visualizations are particularly effective.

- Good times to repeat them are before sleeping and upon waking.

- Whatever thoughts we repeat to ourselves, positive or negative, will become instilled in our subconscious minds and become our reality. Hence, we want to make sure we feed our subconscious with positive thoughts and pictures.

- Affirmations and visualizations are a tool to help us create the life we want.

Exercises

1. Take a normal working day and observe your thoughts. These can be quick glimpses of thoughts or longer monologues or dialogues. Be especially attentive to inner conversations you have with yourself and negative thoughts that pop up. Are you repeating them? For how long? Are they about an important matter? Are they about judging others or yourself?

   At the end of the day, analyze your observances and formulate affirmations on the things that you would like to do or think differently. Make sure that they are phrased in positive terms and note them down, ideally accompanied by visualizations.

   The next morning, start your day with reading these affirmations. Whenever you find yourself trapped in unconstructive negative thinking during the day, stop those thoughts by saying to yourself, "Not now." Then choose to think of something more constructive and meaningful, and bring your attention back to the activity you are doing or that you want to do next. If you like, remind yourself of your affirmations just at that moment. Keep in mind that saying your affirmations once a day but then thinking negatively about the topic the rest of the day will dilute the whole effort, so be mindful so you can catch yourself and pause in those moments of negative thinking.

   Continue this process for three weeks, repeating your affirmations and visualizations frequently, and notice the lasting effects.

2. Take a normal evening and observe what you think about before going to sleep. Are these negative or positive thoughts? In case of the first, try to formulate a positive affirmation. If you cannot find any, just stop the negative thinking by saying, "Not now." Just before you finally sleep, say your affirmation, or think something positive, or just be grateful for whatever you can find to be grateful for. You might agree that this is a much better and more helpful way to end your day.

3. Make it a daily practice to start your day with your affirmations. As things change over time and your goals are fulfilled or become less relevant, come up with new affirmations to continue the positive trend.

Chapter 2

FULFILLING YOUR POTENTIAL

What do I want? Who am I?

The world will ask you who you are, and if you don't know, the world will tell you.
—Carl Gustav Jung

On the way to mastering corporate business life and ultimately creating expanding happiness for ourselves, we need to understand what it means for us to become successful. *Success* is the ability to fulfill our desires, and *true success* is the ability to fulfill our desires with grace and ease. Normally we would think that success only comes with hard work, and the harder the work, the better the results. But *true* success is achieved with a certain ease and joy. Just think of some highly successful people. They often radiate joy and, although they certainly have tough problems to solve, they go about their work with enthusiasm and a sense of play.

Now, a prerequisite to long-lasting success is to know your desires. Sadly, many people do not really know what they want. They may be able to describe what they do *not* want in their lives. However, as we know from the last chapter, this does not have much force. Our subconscious minds work mainly in pictures and terms, and they reinforce what we visualize most. Also, people erroneously think self-confidence is a prerequisite for success. But to be successful, you first and foremost need clarity on what you want and why you want it.

If you lack clarity, you might sometimes have problems staying motivated. Also, not knowing what you want may cause you to complain about things that are not working in your life. And it becomes easy to blame others, because you do not have to act decisively or take responsibility. However, continuously acting like this may quickly weaken or even destroy your success.

Since we are talking about mastering corporate life here, we might think first to measure success in material wealth, but equally important are good physical and mental health, fulfilling relationships, creative freedom, and peace of mind. You might even be at a stage in your career where you already have piled up money only to realize that material possessions are not giving you the happiness and freedom you thought they would.

Since we usually spend a lot of time at work, it would be a pity and overall unfulfilling to seek only private successes. An important aspect of mastering corporate life is being truly successful at work. This means knowing and achieving what you desire in your work and workplace. Hence, first you must know what you want, and then you can formulate goals that will lead you there. Once you have clarity about your goals, your motivation to reach them will be high—as will your chances of achieving them.

Some people may say that instead of stating clear goals, they prefer to be positively surprised by life. If this is you, just realize that chances are high you will then live someone else's life or dream. If you do not know what you want or who you are, then others will tell you. They will interpret on their own what you would probably like to have or who you would want to be, and those assumptions might not be to your liking. One can easily become the plaything of circumstances and the environment.

However, goal setting in corporate environments has been widely studied for decades and we know its effectiveness. Research shows that people who have set goals for themselves, be it at work or in private, are more motivated, which in turn improves their performance and ultimately brings personal wealth (Latham 2017). Done the right way, setting clear goals for yourself will lead to higher performance and greater success.

The first question is "What do I want?"

Of course, your desires will change over time, making success a constantly moving target. Nevertheless, knowing what you want and checking it from time to time is a prerequisite for long-lasting success and happiness.

In order to answer the question of what you truly desire, there are several areas you can turn to:

- Take emotions as your guide. Emotions typically take more information into account than what our rational thoughts can bring together. A good sign is joy. Whenever you feel joy during your day, become aware of what has sparked it. Was it the joy of having completed a difficult analysis, or was it the joy of having brought the right people together to solve a problem? Once you have become aware of what brings you joy, keep it in mind.

- For some people, their most profound dreams reveal what they want to do. Sometimes the dreams repeat and show you various aspects of what you want. Should you have one or multiple such dreams, make sure you write them down to not lose their meanings.

- Think back to when you were a child, about the time you were between seven and fourteen years old. What were you interested in? What did you spend your time doing? What brought you contentment? Your childhood loves might give a hint of what you are genuinely interested in. It might be that you love being together with other people, or thinking deeply on your own, or teaching someone something, or building something futuristic. Whatever it is, do not discount the truth of childhood passions.

- Deep down, you probably know your innermost desire. Some people have desires about what they want to do, but they feel "trapped" in a job for money or due to specific circumstances. They might say that they have a family to support, a mortgage to pay, etc. Regardless of circumstances, knowing your desires is still a good thing. You can analyze the quality of what you would like to do or have, then compare it to the job you are doing today. Typically, you already find qualities in your current job that speak to your desires. The question is whether you find this good enough or whether you want to look for work that is closer to your true desires. In any case, knowing your desires will point you in the right direction.

- You can also gain clarity about what you want by discussing your ideas with people in your network. Whether it is to your sponsor, your mentor, or a business colleague, presenting your idea out loud and hearing their take on it will give you a better idea about it afterwards.

- Lean on your intuition. Intuition is your seventh sense, next to touch, sight, hearing, smell, taste, and the gut feeling that is your unconscious knowledge you can mainly "read" via your emotions. Intuition goes beyond all that. It is information that comes to you even though you have not yet experienced, heard, or read it in your life. Everyone has intuition; some people can just access it more easily. Because you cannot credit it to any source, intuition often has an eccentric connotation in the corporate world, and sometimes managers literally get angry when it is used for problem-solving. However, intuition is often much more precise and directed than logical thinking, as it can handle more information than our reasoning minds. Also, in the corporate world, intuition plays a much bigger part than people are generally aware of. It is something really great inventors and exceptionally successful businesspeople talk about all the time. Albert Einstein said, "All that counts is intuition. The intuitive mind is a gift, and the rational mind is a faithful servant. We have created a society that honors the servant and has forgotten the gift." Or take it from Steve Jobs: "Have the courage to follow your heart and intuition. They somehow already know what you truly want to become. Everything else is secondary."

When you have come up with some idea of your desires, how can you be sure it is really what you want? Whether it is valid and good for you? Here are some questions that might help you validate your answers:

- Does the thing you want to do give you a *sense of purpose*? Do you know why and for whom you are doing it? These are such important considerations that I devoted a separate section after this one to this question of purpose.

- Does it have *growth character*, or a forward movement? If we think back on what we said the purpose of human life is—"the expansion of happiness, and evolution [as] the process through which it is fulfilled"—we understand that we can judge every desire by whether it has the potential for evolution or growth. Every living being on this planet grows. If it does not grow, it will shrink and die. Therefore, if your goal leads to progress, most probably it is a worthy and sustainable goal.

- Does it bring you into *flow*? The incredibly valuable concept of flow is described by Mihaly Csikszentmihalyi in his book *Flow* (1990). It is defined as a state of complete immersion in an activity, where your whole being is involved and you are using your skills to the utmost. You can get into flow when the challenges you face match your skills. If your skills are not enough for the challenges you face, you get worried or anxious. If the challenges are too low for your skills, you become relaxed, then bored, down to apathetic. People achieving a state of flow report being completely involved in a task. They are totally absorbed by it without their attention straying to any distracting thoughts. What they feel, wish, and think are in harmony. Often the activity seems to be effortless, and people are fully living in the moment. Hours seem to pass in minutes. Typically, obtaining flow leads to feelings of satisfaction, fulfillment, and happiness. People who work in a state of flow have an intense awareness of life and feel that their life is worth living.

- Does it have an *element of creativity*? People are very often content when they get to create something. This does not mean you need to paint or craft a masterpiece. Solving a problem, introducing a new process at work, or contributing to some new feature of the business all require a lot of creativity.

- What does it *do for others*? Instead of asking ourselves what our own interests and passions are, we should focus more on what we can do for others to make the world a better place. In my opinion, this is the most important consideration. If you like what you do and do it to help others, it almost guarantees your own happiness and success. Remember the universal "law of giving and receiving" from the first chapter: If you want success, the surest way to get it is to give it.

The more important question is "Who am I?"

Figuring out what you really want is one thing. However, spiritual leaders and psychologists alike have taught us that on our journey, it is more important to focus on who we are becoming and what legacy we may leave behind rather than what we have or want to get.

In order to answer that question, again, there are several areas you can turn to:

- Look inwards and reflect on your true self—your aspirations, hopes, and fears.

- Know your own values. I find this so important that I dedicate a section to it later in this chapter.

- There are some well-proven personality questionnaires that can bring you insights about your personality traits. Here is a list of some renowned tests, some of which are even freely available on the internet:

  - VIA (Values In Action) Signature Strength test: This free self-assessment comprises 240 questions to help you understand your best qualities. This test is based on the book *Authentic Happiness* (2004) by Dr. Seligman, in which he describes these qualities and gives actionable tips to apply the strengths of each for finding greater well-being.

- Big Five Personality Traits: The test measures the five personality traits of extraversion, agreeableness, conscientiousness, emotional stability, and openness to experience. These five traits represent five categories of individual characteristics that, taken together, describe patterns of thoughts, feelings, and behaviors. In addition to the main traits, many Big Five questionnaires also measure various subcomponents of each trait. The test is very popular with personality psychologists, as people's scores tend to be consistent, and predictions made using this model are reproducible. Also, the selection of the traits has been done in a very systematic and comprehensive fashion.

- StrengthsFinder 2.0: This test focuses on your strengths rather than your preferences or behaviors. It identifies your top 5 out of 34 possible strengths. It also gives strategies on how to leverage your strengths for improved performance. Each strength comes with ideas for action and how to work with others who share that strength. The positive psychology theory behind this test is based on the belief that we should not focus on our weaknesses but on our natural strengths and build on what we do best. It is a great way to better understand how you approach work and striving toward your goals.

Some critics of such tests argue that they tend to categorize people into too few categories, or that there is confirmation bias, where people have the tendency to give more weight to questions about things they like about their personality and assign less weight to those pointing to less favorable traits. However, the assessments presented here have addressed these reservations to a large degree and have been designed with care. In any case, these tests provide you with a vocabulary to inspire you on your inner search for what makes you, you.

- Observing the good in your friends is another way to figure out who you are. Some people say that your qualities are about the average of the qualities of the five people you spend the most time with. And by the universal "law of mirrors," we understand that our friends mirror qualities we have in us.

If you really want to dig deep in finding out who you are, you need a real sense of awareness. On the one hand, you can learn a lot by observing how you interact with others. You need to be aware of yourself in relationships, discover how you act and react, what inputs and responses you give. On the other hand, you need stillness and introspection. Certainly, meditation will help bring you back to who you are at your innermost core. Also, repeatedly asking yourself the question "Who am I?" will bring you insight. Just listen to every small whisper you hear from within you.

Sometimes it takes a while to understand what you really want and who you really are. Maybe it takes years to realize why you chose a certain profession. Some of us may never have consciously thought about it in the ways described above. Doing so is not absolutely necessary if you are happy and content in your professional and personal life. However, if you still see room to become a happier, more fulfilled person, then asking yourself what you really want and who you really are is certainly a good thing.

ANSWERING THE QUESTION "WHAT DO I WANT?"

Many years back, when I was in grammar school, we all had a "sports week" to attend a movement class of our choosing and I was assigned to my second choice: jazz dance. I was quite disappointed because I did not enjoy jazz dance nearly as much as the first sport I had chosen. Nevertheless, the sports week turned out to be quite enjoyable, not because of jazz dance but because I got to spend a week together with my friends. At the end of the week, I thought about the two teachers and to my full astonishment, I said to myself, "That is what I would like to do when I grow up." Back then, it was a mystery for me why I would want to do this, as I really did not like jazz dance that much. Then, too soon, I forgot the thought entirely. Years later, I realized that the teachers sparked a joy in me that showed me what I wanted to do in my life—I wanted to pursue leadership. Yes, I wanted to become a leader. I wanted to organize things for others, teach them, and give them a great experience. When I led my first team, many years later, it was like coming home. I realized then that this was the piece in my life that had been missing so far, and I truly understood that spark of joy I discovered way back in this sports week.

Figuring out what you want and who you are is obviously a process and probably a lifelong experience because circumstances change, as do our goals. However, answering those questions for yourself at any time will make you more self-aware. You will feel more authentic, engaged, and confident. And chances are, you will have greater success and will feel more satisfaction and happiness as a result.

Summary

- Success is the ability to fulfill our desires. In order to be successful, we first need to get clarity on our desires.

- There are multiple ways of finding out what we want for our work life. Thinking about our deepest desires, noticing specific activities and tasks that spark joy, and talking with mentors or colleagues are just a few examples.

- We can be sure about what we want if our desires have a growth character or bring us into flow. Also, if the thing we want to do contributes to a larger whole, in particular if it helps other people, then we can deem the desire worthy and valid.

- Even more important is to know who we are. To find out our own strengths and values, we can turn to personality questionnaires. Studying the qualities of our friends will give insight too.

Exercises

1. Make a "mind map" of what you want and who you are. Take a sheet of paper, write your name in the middle, and draw lines outward in all directions. At the other end of each line, write one of the following categories: family, relationships, work life, leisure, finances, career, properties, health, spirituality. For each category, write keywords about what you have or want, your interests, who you are, your qualities, and your characteristics. Then, for each category, think about what is particularly important for you. Make notes on what you would like to advance and achieve. As we are talking about *corporate* life mastery in this book, do this in detail for the categories of your work life and career. What would you like to further explore or clarify? Try to write it down in the form of goals.

2. For a whole work week, become attentive to your emotions. Every time you feel joy, reflect on what has sparked this joy and write it down. At the end of the week, review the list and look for any patterns.

   If you can remember them, add to the list past experiences at work where you felt similar joy or a deep desire to do something new. This will greatly increase your self-awareness as well as your self-confidence.

   You can also do this with other types of feelings, such as less positive ones like anger, envy, or disappointment. Whenever you feel a spark of something, pause for a moment and notice it, then examine it closely as if under a magnifying glass. In the best case, you will also find some unnecessary negative thoughts that you can directly replace with supportive ones (see exercises in chapter 1).

Finding purpose and meaning

Only a life lived for others is worth living.

—Albert Einstein

In his book *Flourish* (2011), psychologist Dr. Seligman summarizes decades of empirical research on what really makes people happy and satisfied in their lives. He presents two key factors: "achievement and doing what is valuable."

The first factor, *achievement,* sometimes called mastery, means becoming really good at something. The second factor, also called purpose or meaning, means that you strive to do something for a reason greater than just making yourself happy.

With the first factor, most people have a relatively good idea of what skills they have or want to acquire. Now, if unsure what further skills to acquire, we can turn to the second factor and ask ourselves what we would like to do that is valuable. Then we can choose whether or not to acquire the required skills.

Some people say you should follow your passions. However, I have observed several times with others and myself that passion can follow learning and can be found in applying new skills. We did not know beforehand that we would enjoy working with these new skills so much. Sometimes, even learning these skills was not much fun. But once something is mastered, the joy and deep interest for it began. However, your current passions can, of course, show you what skills and purpose to pursue.

When it comes to the second factor, people often have more difficulty understanding how to find *meaning or purpose.* Purpose is the reason *why* you do what you do. It is the true motivation for your actions and efforts in life. Knowing your purpose gives your life a direction and keeps you focused. You will live with conviction, and life becomes more meaningful. Research has shown that finding and living out one's purpose is associated with a longer life. Studies have even concluded that having a purpose—and finding it—is as important for longevity as living a healthy lifestyle.

Some spiritual leaders say that every life has its own purpose to fulfill. They claim that everyone has a unique gift or talent to express in this world. As much as I like the idea and find it beautiful, figuring out one's unique gift tends to be a rather difficult undertaking. The search for your true calling can be endless and carries with it an enormous pressure to find something original and unique.

Research has a good answer to this conundrum. It has been found that it is not so important what the purpose of a person's life is, but that they have one. Hence, going forward, we will concentrate on finding purpose in your work life, rather than your one and only unique life's purpose—which might very well be the same thing for some. For instance, you might find that your unique life purpose is to be a good mother to your children, but you work for a company too. Then you might find your purpose at work is training and mentoring younger employees. In this example, to work it out fully, you could conclude that your unique life purpose might be around developing people in general.

Finding your purpose

Now, a short way to find *your purpose* is to answer the following questions:

- Who are you?

- What do you do?

- Why do you do it?

- Who will benefit other than you?

- Why will they benefit?

- How will they change because of you?

These questions are sometimes just the beginning of your search for purpose. However, even if you have not fully found it through this exercise, these questions have certainly already led you in the right direction. If you need further guidance, you can ask yourself the following additional questions:

- What do I enjoy most at work? What do I look forward to doing? What activity brings me the most satisfaction? What activity would I like to spend most of my time doing?

- What are my strongest skills? What am I good at doing? What are my unique talents? At work, what takes me the least effort? What task am I given because I am the best person to do it? What have others noticed about my skills?

- What kind of contribution do I want to make? What makes me feel useful? At work, what makes me most proud?

- How do I relate to others? What would I like to contribute for others? What types of working partnerships are best suited for me? How would I describe my ideal work colleagues and business partners?

- Where do I want to grow? In what areas do I want to make progress? What next steps would I like to take? How does my current work help me advance to where I would like to end up?

- What do I want to be seen for? What do I want to convey? What legacy would I like to leave behind?

There is a great deal of literature out there about how to find one's purpose. If you want to dive deep and find purpose for yourself or your team in a very structured way, I can highly recommend *Find Your Why* by Simon Sinek et al. (2017).

Another very nice book on the topic is *Ikigai* by Héctor García and Francesc Miralles (2016). It explains the Japanese secret to a long and happy life through finding and living your *ikigai*, your "reason of being." Ikigai is described as the intersection of: "what you love," "what you are good at," "what the world needs," and "what you can be paid for." It encompasses your passion, your profession, your mission, and your vocation. The authors say that we each have an ikigai deep within ourselves and that finding it requires a patient search. However, once found, it makes people keep doing what they love for as long as their health allows. As such, it is a major prerequisite for a long life.

Having a sense of purpose at work makes us feel that what we do matters. In fact, the sense of meaning that employees derive from purposeful work translates into elevated levels of engagement. And along with the individual benefits of better health, more contentment, and ultimately higher happiness, companies see economic benefit as well.

You might yourself think, or you may have employees who think, that they mainly work for money and find their purpose outside of work. For individuals with this mindset, I recommend digging deeper. You might unearth aspects of your work where you can find purpose. Sometimes, a shift in perspective can make a job purposeful.

The purpose you find in your work may also change over time. What you find particularly purposeful when you are 20 years old may not be the same when you are 40 or 50 years old.

In any case, the closer you live in accordance with your true purpose, the healthier and happier your life will be. People who live their lives contrary to what they believe in and what they are interested in may attract sickness or end up burning themselves out.

FINDING MEANING

When I was about 40, after having worked many long and hard hours over a longer time span, sometimes even working whole weekends, I started to question why I was doing it at all. Thinking about our clients who wanted to optimize their profits with some structured insurance transaction, I wondered whether my time was really well spent in this world, or whether there was something more useful waiting for me to put my efforts toward. In other words, I lacked a sense of purpose.

At that time, many of my friends had advanced in their careers. One friend was working in an important communication position at UNICEF; another one was giving legal advice at Human Rights Watch. You can understand why I felt I was lacking meaning in my position. However, I had a very wise manager at the time, and he gave me his thoughts and elaborated on what insurance, and in particular the insurance field I was working in, did to stabilize the financial system and ultimately what it did for mankind. After this profound talk, I felt much better, and after some further thinking, I was able to find real meaning in my life and my work.

FINDING PURPOSE

Another example of purpose tied to fulfillment came in conjunction with a mentee's wish to get promoted. She was a young mother of two children and a diligent and high-performing employee. When she first came to me, she had just lost a promotion to a colleague and was quite demotivated, as she felt she would have been a much better candidate. As I talked with her to find out why she really desired the promotion, we discovered that most of the aspects she expected the new position to give her could already be found in her current role. It was liberating for her to find meaning in her current position, and according to her manager, she actually performed even better after the coaching session with me.

WHOM DOES YOUR WORK SERVE?

Another example from business life, which concerns the search for purpose and the underlying question of whom your work serves: A colleague, who used to be very successful, once attended a personal development course about finding his purpose. I suspect that he attended this course because he had recently been laid off. When asked about what drives him, he claimed that he did not care about any people except for his family, and certainly not for people in the corporate environment. He claimed that the only thing that really meant anything to him was the content of his work—the subject area he specialized in. In his spare time, he gave lectures to people about his hobby, and there, too, he claimed that he was only concerned about the subject at hand. Ironically, this colleague was not self-aware enough to realize that while he claimed to only care about the topics, he was spending valuable time teaching *people* through his lectures, sharing his knowledge and passion. If he was only concerned about the subject matter, he would not have bothered to give lectures to teach others.

In summary, it makes sense to ask yourself the question "Who will benefit other than you and why?" to help you find your purpose.

Sometimes it takes a while to figure out your purpose. However, once you have formulated it, you will be able to check where you are in relation to it today. You will probably realize that you are already well positioned with where you currently are working. Knowing your purpose will also show you what direction your next steps should be as you go along your career path. Alternatively, you may also find that your current job is not directly geared towards fulfilling your purpose. In that case, you might want to either discuss whether your current role can be adjusted, or you might want to search for a different job that is closer to what your heart desires.

If your heart harbors desires that lie outside the work you are currently doing, ask yourself the following questions:

- Why do I want to fulfill the desire of my heart?

- What do I gain by fulfilling this desire of my heart?

- What would I have to sacrifice or what would I lose if this desire of my heart were to be fulfilled?

- What are the effects on me, my family, my work, my friends, society, etc.?

To answer the above questions clearly, you need honesty towards yourself. You might have a hundred excuses for why your desires are unfulfilled, but also true restrictions. To learn the difference, you may want to answer the following questions:

- What prevents you from living your purpose?

- Do you worry about what others would say?

- Do you fear failure?

- Do you try to please everyone and do justice to all and everything?

- Are you waiting for inspiration?

- Are your objections excuses or real restrictions?

- Are you lacking certain skills, or are certain behaviors holding you back? If so, what, if anything, can be done in these areas?

- What would be the best possible alternative to your original purpose and desire, taking your restrictions into account?

For most of the people who come to the end of this line of questioning and find that they cannot live their purpose in their current work, the last question is the most profound. Deciding that they want to make a change is a big ask, as most people are in the middle of a busy life full of obligations, responsibilities, and other daily demands. Making a completely new life oftentimes exceeds people's possibilities and is probably too overwhelming. However, little changes in the right direction may bring you more slowly but surely toward your purpose.

In any case, knowing your purpose helps you define your goals. As you remember from the last section, every action should be in the evolutionary direction and in the direction of progress. Formulating goals works best when they are action-oriented rather than outcome-oriented. For example, it is better to write "I will learn a new skill and then ask for a promotion" than simply "I will get a promotion." Also, make sure the goals you pursue are reasonable and under your control.

Living your full potential

Now, knowing your purpose and your goals towards fulfilling it, the question remains: Are you living your full potential? The answer has to do with how big you think. Living your full potential requires you to set bold goals that will bring you there. But do not be discouraged; even if you have not yet reached your full potential, you may already feel fulfillment along the way, as fulfillment is doing what you like and find meaningful.

In my opinion, even your full potential is something that expands over time. The closer you come to fulfilling your potential, the more your potential will expand. In other words, theoretically, your potential is unlimited.

Living your purpose will certainly bring you in the direction of living your full potential. Sometimes, this takes courage and confidence. Oftentimes, it just takes an awareness of what you want, the formulation of explicit goals, and the discipline to follow them. However, the force behind having a purpose is immense. If you tap into that force, you will easily meet your targets.

Some people have only a vague idea about their purpose. This does not mean that they cannot live a fulfilling life. They may live their purpose without spelling it out for themselves. Even so, chances are it takes them more energy to stay motivated than if they had a clearer picture to direct their efforts.

Some people's mindset prevents them from reaching their full potential, and they first must become aware and then let go of limiting beliefs. This will certainly make them more self-confident, as we already saw in chapter 1.

Another possibility is that people are not living their potential. If that's the case, they may experience regrets, or complain about how things should have been, or feel pain, or even become hopeless and depressed. They may be functional but not fulfilled. At best, they may be outwardly successful but not satisfied.

In any case, once you have your goals set, you need to take action. If you are torn between options, chose the one that brings you the most joy, and then force yourself to act. Achieving this chosen goal will become your top priority. In case it does not work out, you at least will have learned something. Only through concrete action do things become manifest. It is useless to have knowledge if you do not apply it. Often, we wait for some kind of permission or invitation from outside to get us into action. However, it is important to realize that the responsibility to ignite change lies *within ourselves* and only we can fulfill our intentions through concrete action. Whenever you take action, ask yourself whether it is going in the direction you want.

I cannot stress enough that when we bring value to work with our own unique skills and talents, when we do things for others, which brings progress, we will get rewarded, materially, emotionally, and spiritually. To do this for a whole work lifetime, you need motivation, which you will be getting for free if you are doing personally purposeful work—work that matters to you, that is aligned with who you are, and fulfills what your heart desires. Work with purpose will keep you energized and will make you effective and productive.

Summary

- Two factors make people happy and satisfied in their lives: achievement and doing what is valuable.

- High achievement, also called mastery, means becoming really good at something.

- Doing what is valuable to us means finding meaning, also called purpose.

- Having a sense of purpose at work makes people feel that what they do matters. It leads to better health and more contentment at work. It translates into elevated levels of engagement, and with that, companies see economic benefit too.

- Knowing our purpose helps us define goals that guide us along our career path.

Exercises

1. Following the questions and guidance in this section, find your purpose for your work life. Compare it to your current work. Are there parts of your purpose which are missing in your current work? Try to formulate goals that lead you in the direction of your purpose and write them down. Note that written goals are more powerful. Writing them down greatly increases your chances of achieving them because your focus will be sharpened, and your daily actions will be aligned. Re-read these goals regularly, at least once or twice a week. This will increase your sense of purpose in your life.

2. Think about how your position within your company contributes to

your company's purpose statement. Does your company's mission align with your own thinking? It may be that you work in a support function, such as finance or information technology, and that your work content is not directly related to your company's unique purpose. In my opinion, it is still important that you feel some personal alignment with your company's purpose. Otherwise, you may lose meaning over time.

Know your own values

Keep your values positive, because your values become your destiny.
—Mahatma Gandhi

Our personal values are a set of beliefs and qualities we strive to live by. We hold these beliefs and qualities in very high importance, but they are not innate and can even change over time. They mainly come from our environment and are shaped by education, upbringing, and life experiences. Our personal values are what motivate us in our lives, even if we are not always aware of them. As human beings, it is important to us that we live by our values. To feel satisfied, we need to perceive our life as worthy and principled, as something valuable. If we live according to our values, we are in harmony with ourselves and we feel content and satisfied. If our behavior is misaligned with our values, we may feel purposeless, frustrated, and unhappy. If our values are violated, we suddenly feel uncomfortable and that something is wrong. In those cases, we can better understand our dissatisfaction if we know our values. Thereby, knowing our basic values also makes it easier to get satisfaction in life.

As an example, if honesty is an important value to you, you will probably be bitterly disappointed if you are lied to. If family is important to you, a weekend relationship because of your work is probably out of the question. For some people, a high-flying career is important, while others attach more importance to a secure job.

Personal values vary greatly between cultures and individuals, for example honesty, freedom, security, reliability, recognition, creativity, or perhaps wealth and power. Sometimes it is easier to name things we do not want or no longer want than it is to come up with a list of our values from scratch. However, knowing your values might ease your life, especially the larger decisions that determine the trajectory of your career.

To determine your own values, you can ask yourself the following questions:

- What is generally important in life?

- What is important to me?

- What do I prefer to spend my time on?

- What would I miss if I no longer had it?

- What would I pay money to do?

- When am I proud of myself?

- When do I feel uncomfortable?

- What do I value and admire about my friends?

- What kind of behavior can I not tolerate?

- What is the most important thing in my job?

The above questions should lead you to articulate certain values that are important to you. If you want to consider things another way, make a list of values that come to your mind when you think about different areas of life, such as *family, partnership, friends, work, health, finances*, as well as your *emotional, intellectual*, and *spiritual life*. Write down at least three values per area.

Below are some ideas of commonly held values to get you started. These lists are not meant to be exhaustive, and keep in mind that sometimes we hold certain values without real reflection because most of society seems to accept them. However, you might have other important values that you hold personally that do not appear below, and you should definitely write those down as well.

Job: achievement, ambition, appreciation, authority, challenge, community, competence, contribution, cooperation, creativity, curiosity, development, employment security, experiences, financial security, growth, harmony, independence, influence, knowledge, leadership, meaningful work, power, recognition, relationships, reputation, respect, responsibility, service, speed, stability, status, success, training, wealth

Family/friends: acceptance, attractiveness, belonging, compassion, equality, family, fidelity, friendship, helpfulness, humanity, love, loyalty, reliability

Yourself: adventure, authenticity, autonomy, balance, beauty, boldness, calmness, confidence, courage, determination, fairness, faith, fame, freedom, fun, generosity, happiness, health, honesty, humor, integrity, joy, justice, kindness, learning, openness, optimism, peace, personal growth, pleasure, poise, politeness, popularity, religion, satisfaction, self-control, self-expression, self-realization, self-respect, social standing, spirituality, tolerance, trustworthiness, well-being, wisdom

After your reflections, you should have a list of about 10 to 20 values. Now, take all the values you listed and roughly sort them by importance. An effective way to prioritize your value list is by using a technique called pairwise comparison analysis. This method is typically used for working out the relative importance of several different options. It works as follows:

1. Create a table where you list your values once from top to bottom and again in the same order from left to right. You now have a two-dimensional matrix.

2. Starting from the top left, take the first value and compare it to each of the values listed down the first column. Put a 1 in the field where the value on top is more important than the value you are comparing it to on the left, otherwise put a 0 in that field.

3. When you have filled the column, copy these values over to complete the first row, by transposing and exchanging the values. This means you need to take then a 0 for a 1 and vice versa. You have now filled the first column and the first row.

4. Do the same for each value across the top row. Always, after filling a column, fill the rest of the row by transposing and exchanging the values, except for the field with the same value.

5. After having filled the whole table, except the diagonal fields (comparison of same values), add up the numbers in each column of the table and write them in the bottom line. The highest sum in this line is your top value, the second highest sum your second most important value, and so on. In case you have a tie, see how the two values scored against each other in the table. The one you assessed as more important is then the higher priority.

If you had difficulty following these instructions, you can find free templates on the internet for pairwise comparison analysis.

I really recommend prioritizing your values such that you can come up with your top five values. I recommend not taking more than five core values to focus on. If you have too many, nothing is a priority anymore. Note down your top five values and whenever you encounter an uneasy situation, you can weigh it against your value system and use these values to help you navigate your way through. This will accelerate the solution greatly.

Conflicts with others or between groups often arise from differences in value systems. The more you are aware of your own values, the more you can react properly and directly influence the situation.

Values change over time. At the beginning of our career, our values might be focused on our own growth and getting as much as we can, whereas later in our lives, we perhaps stop asking "What is in it for me?" and have more values around how to serve society. As we move beyond this phase, towards the end of life, people tend to have values that are more spiritual in nature.

Values can even be consciously changed when we choose to work on ourselves. In particular, if your values are limiting you, you might want to broaden your views. For example, if from your upbringing you are very parsimonious, you might be less generous than you would like to be. Hence, you can decide to become more generous. You do this by first starting with a clear decision that you want to change and then applying it whenever you can, starting with small things like being generous with your compliments, for example. Little by little, you open yourself to larger acts of generosity and you will see how much more generous the world will be to you. If this is very important to you, you will be able to do it.

In general, it is of great importance that you live your values. If you do not, in the long run, you might become unhappy, feel unfulfilled, and even fall ill, as living against your beliefs causes subconscious stress. Hence, under no circumstances should you change your values to suit someone else. Sometimes, hard choices will need to be made. For example, if you have opposite values to your manager and you feel that your own values are constantly being violated, it may be best for you to move on.

Summary

- Our values are the set of beliefs and qualities we strive to live by. These beliefs and qualities are very important to us as human beings.

- Values are not innate; they can change over time. Also, we can choose to work on ourselves and consciously change our values.

- We can list our values by answering some specific questions. We can find our top values by prioritizing our list using pairwise comparison analysis.

- Living by our values is a prerequisite for contentment in life.

Exercises

1. Make a list of your top five values utilizing the process described above.

Pick one value from time to time, for instance one per day, and try to live by it that day. You will feel happiness as a result.

2. Think about how your values have changed over time. Did their priority change over time, or did you perhaps attain new values? Are there values you would like to de-prioritize? With what value would you like to substitute them? Think about how you can do this in your actions.

3. Reflect on the values of your manager. Would you guess that your top values are on your manager's top-five list? If not, think about how you will deal with problems that might arise in this regard later. In any case, keep your values high and be proud of them.

On being yourself

Be yourself; everyone else is already taken.

—Oscar Wilde

It should go without saying that when you know what you want and who you are—or when living your purpose—you cannot neglect yourself. In corporate life I have seen people far too often try to be someone they genuinely are not. For instance, they might always act loud and tough, when inside they were quite agreeable people. They thought they needed to be like this so that others would understand what they want and because this was the general tone in that department. However, this made them inauthentic. You could even tell that they did not feel very comfortable with it, and you did not get the impression they were happy either.

In fact, by pretending to be someone they thought would be the ideal person for the job or the position they aspired to in the future, they negated who they truly are.

However, negating yourself for the benefit of doing a job will never make you happy. It will also not make you successful in the long run.

Oftentimes, people who pretend also change what they say—their "story"—depending on what they think each person wants to hear. This typically takes up an incredible amount of their energy, as they need to keep their different stories straight.

In any case, if people do not act as themselves for a long time, they usually become very unhappy. They have no peace of mind, and, at worst, they might grow exhausted, leading to serious illnesses and depression. Just remember, we spend too much time at work to only be ourselves in the time we are not working.

The desire to shape ourselves to fit a different mold comes from constant comparisons with others. Comparing ourselves with others tends to lower our self-esteem and makes us feel bad about ourselves. It comes from the constant need to assign valuation. Many people go through the world always judging their environment as "good" or "bad" and thinking about what others should or should not be doing. This is an incredible waste of time and energy and pulls them away from who they are. Just think about the time and energy you gain if you do not have to think about whether you find the weather good or bad, or whether you like someone or not. The same goes with your neighbors, people next to you in public transportation, colleagues, culture, politics, pop culture, and others' views and opinions. Just take things as they are, and you will be more relaxed, freeing up time and energy for things that are important to you.

This does not mean to become disinterested or indifferent. On the contrary, you can focus your energy where you need to make sound judgements. You will have much more clarity for these activities and will recognize the important things more easily.

Also, you should stop thinking about what others think about you, and you should not try to be what you think others want you to be. Look at it this way: On the one hand, it is intrusive to wonder what others think. You actually have "no right" to look into others' minds. On the other hand, you should not live someone else's life. Hence, you should really not care about what others are thinking at all.

Putting aside comparison with others requires a conscious effort to stop caring about others' opinions of us. Likewise, you should stop passing judgement on what others should or should not be doing. It all starts with the decision to stop such behavior and then be attentive if you find yourself thinking this way again. In those moments, remind yourself of your decision.

The less you judge other people, the less you judge yourself and the more you can stand by yourself and be who you really are.

This all does not exclude working on your character. If you feel someone has a great leadership style that you would like to emulate, watch that person and learn from them. Then practice the behaviors and traits you observed until they become a part of yourself. However, if it does not feel comfortable and genuine to you, you should let it go, otherwise you risk neglecting yourself.

BEING TRUE TO YOURSELF

For several years, I organized mentoring sessions for young businesswomen. I once had a participant, a wonderful young woman of African descent. You could guess that she came from a very different background than the others. However, she was particularly well adapted to business life and tried not to unduly stand out. When I talked about "being yourself" at work, she was amazed that this was even possible. She apparently believed that you had to fit in. I encouraged her to think about it and bring more of herself to the workplace. I was convinced that she could bring a sought-after diversity of thought to the workplace and be even more valuable to her team and the company.

In the corporate world, too, you get to be you. Even more, you *need* to be yourself! In the corporate environment, companies are typically searching for diverse teams for better and faster problem-solving. How can you deliver your fullest when you are not yourself? Moreover, everyone trying to offer similar opinions and similar ideas does not bring the necessary diversity in thinking that makes decisions stronger and innovations better.

At the same time, please do not confuse being yourself with simply saying everything that comes to your mind right away or letting out every emotion you feel. This is definitely not useful, as your raw thoughts or emotions might not contribute meaningfully to the topics discussed and could even be harmful if your unfiltered words are unkind to others. So, while staying honest to your own beliefs and values, try always to be thoughtful and sensitive of how you present your ideas to others.

Anyhow, your genuine self is the most precious resource you have. You cannot give up character for the sake of a job or someone else's approval. You really need to respect yourself. And it goes without saying that you need to think highly of yourself, independent of whether you believe someone else thinks that you might not be good enough.

You need to remind yourself who you are, with all your strengths, weaknesses, knowledge, skills, and opportunity areas. The more aware you are of this, the more you can appreciate who you are. Do not judge yourself in comparison to others; at best, compare yourself to you in earlier times. Set your own expectations of yourself and work on them, following your own thoughts and your own intuition, and try your best to live up to them. You will feel good about yourself, you will have greater courage, compassion, and authenticity, and you will become self-confident and fulfilled with peace of mind.

Summary

- It costs us an incredible amount of energy not to be ourselves. Not only is it counterproductive, but it is also exhausting to act against our true selves for a long period of time.

- Putting on acts and facades comes from constant comparison with others. People tend to categorize people and things into "good" and "bad." This judgement is a waste of time and energy.

- Being ourselves makes us feel good about ourselves and gives us greater courage, compassion, and authenticity. It is a secure way to be more self-confident and fulfilled with peace of mind.

Exercises

1. If you sometimes struggle with being yourself, start a daily practice of expressing yourself. You can start with simple things, such as wearing a certain piece of clothing that you particularly like but is not too common in your workplace, or expressing your opinion during the coffee break. From there, try expressing your opinion in meetings, especially if it brings in a different point of view. By expressing your uniqueness on a daily basis, you will become more confident and assertive and ultimately feel more comfortable and fulfilled.

2. If you find it difficult to say "no," prepare pre-written answers on small notecards to questions so that you have them immediately at hand when someone asks you to do something you do not have time for, or to express an opinion you do not want to express, or to do something you just do not want to do. For example, "I have to think about it," or "Maybe next time, since I'm really busy." The more you stand by yourself, the easier it will be for you to not compromise as often. Additionally, you will find that the more you stand up for yourself, the less people will think to ask things of you or assign you something you do not want to do.

3. For one day, try to become aware of how often you make valuations. How often do you judge something or someone? It might be twice an hour, or it could well be twice a minute. Think about whether it does you any good to judge, and how you might think about the person or situation in a neutral way instead.

Chapter 3

ON SELF-MANAGEMENT

On self-positioning

If you don't design your own life plan, chances are you'll fall into someone else's plan. And guess what they have planned for you? Not much.

—Jim Rohn

Everyone is a manager and a leader because you are managing and leading yourself. The more consciously you are doing it, the better. Corporate life mastery starts with mastering yourself. This means mastering your thoughts, your emotions, and your activities. You learned in the chapters before how your thoughts and emotions can be managed for positive gain. Coming to activities, we can master them and direct them when we know what we want in our lives, which we figured out in the previous chapter. With a clear and calm mind, you will find out what you want and who you *actually* are. By consciously choosing goals, you will be able to reach what you want to achieve and become who you truly want to be.

Achieving goals means being successful in pursuit of what you want. This is fully in line with what life is meant to be: Expanding happiness. That is why working towards goals is important. If you have no goals, you will just aimlessly drift along, ending up somewhere others want you to go, like a leaf on a lake. You easily become the plaything of others, and finding a sense of meaningful accomplishment is less likely. However, having established your goals and set action plans accordingly, be grateful for every small step on your way and celebrate any achievement.

Now, self-positioning is in fact nothing more than evaluating yourself by finding out what you want to achieve, setting goals to get there, and ultimately realizing who you are or want to be—or, as some people say, setting your personal brand. Doing this will help you to navigate complex and constantly changing business environments.

Wise goal setting

Let us first talk about goal setting and then proceed to personal branding. Usually, goal setting consists of two elements. First, you need a long-term vision that is ambitious and makes you dream. There is no specific time horizon, but you can think about five or more years into the future. Your vision could be to live out the purpose we talked about in the last chapter. Second, you need a concrete mid-term plan that will help you make decisions toward your long-term vision. Again, the exact time horizon is not that important. You can think about 12 to 18 months. Both the long-term vision and mid-term goals need to be written down as clearly as possible. When you note down your expectations, they become much more real and tangible. This will help you stay focused and motivated. The best way to formulate your goals is to write what you want to do, why, and for whom. This can be as simple as, for example, "I do X so that Y, and it helps many people to do Z."

Please remember from the first chapter, your goals need to be positively formulated. If you can make them visual, even better, to make it easy for your subconscious mind to support them. Never formulate something in a negative way. Sentences like "I want to stop X" or "I don't want to have Y" will most probably not work. They do not have the right energy, and your subconscious mind will absorb the idea without the negation. Hence you might get exactly what you did *not* want.

Also, do not be scared to reach for the stars. As Michelangelo wrote centuries ago, "The greater danger for most of us lies not in setting our aim too high and falling short but in setting our aim too low and achieving our mark." In fact, if you set your goals too low, you risk not reaching your full potential, which would be a huge pity. While your goals should be *big*, they somehow also need to be *achievable*. You do not need to know right now exactly how you will reach your goals, but you do need, especially for your mid-term goals, to have the feeling that you can achieve them somehow. Just remember, when you wish something from your deepest heart, it will be achievable for you.

Additionally, make sure you have only a few but clearly formulated goals, otherwise you run the risk of spreading yourself too thin and not making progress or feeling uncertain about too many goals. As mentioned earlier, make sure you write down your goals. If you do not write down a goal, it is more likely to remain a wish or a dream that can change at any moment. It is also helpful if you link your goals back to your purpose and answer for yourself: Why do you want to achieve this goal? Who will benefit if you achieve this goal and why? Your answers to these questions will give you meaningful reasons to achieve your goals. Also, write your goals in the present tense, as if they have already been reached. Make them as real and tangible as possible—your mind will understand what you are trying to accomplish.

The more excited you are about your goals, the higher the chances that you will achieve them. To recap: Your goals should ideally be written down, positively formulated and visualized, slightly overexaggerated but still achievable, and give you a great sense of excitement.

Meaningful action plans

In order to achieve a goal, you need to create a *meaningful action plan* and follow through. You need discipline and persistence to work towards your goals. For your mid-term goals, it might help to think about how it feels to have achieved one of them. Then formulate the last step that was needed to get there. Work your way back step by step and imagine what was needed to achieve each little milestone. If you have worked all the way back, you should literally get your first step, or your to-do right now. Make sure this first step is easy to achieve and doable in the near future so that you can celebrate your first success soon.

You may have goals for which making a concrete action plan is not that easy, and you will only know what to do next when you are on your way. In that case, it helps to have a strong long-term goal to propel you. In the end, prioritize your goals by what is most important for you to achieve and put a focus on those.

In any case, chances are high that what you write down as your goals will come to fruition. This is not only because you will make conscious decisions that will move you in the direction of your long-term vision—your North Star, as some people call it—but also because your subconscious mind will do things and make tiny decisions in that direction as well.

Writing down your goals makes you accountable and gives you the necessary self-discipline to move forward. Remember from chapter 1: Life is about happiness in conjunction with expansion and progress, and nothing makes you as satisfied and happy as progress in something you feel is valuable and helps others. Let your North Star guide you to make progress. For every important decision you have to make, ask yourself this as a guiding principle: Does it bring you forward to the fulfillment of your goals or not?

By consciously choosing your goals, you will not spin your wheels, procrastinate, or stand still for long. Hence, it greatly helps to manage your time and productivity.

After having established goals and action plans, you must make sure to take steps forward. Everyone knows that goals can never be achieved without action. Every journey starts with the first step and each step, even the smallest action, will ultimately determine your success.

In my corporate mentoring life, I saw people who, although having set inspiring and reasonable goals for themselves, did not take the necessary steps towards fulfilling them. Either they waited for someone to give them permission or for some inspiration to strike. In these cases, it helped when people made a commitment to themselves to grow almost on a daily basis. In some cases, they just needed to get clearer and more specific in their action plans and their priorities. Other times, though, what got people going was the realization that they needed to sacrifice short-term pleasure for opportunity. In that case or any situation where someone was lacking commitment, reminding themselves of the higher goals and their purpose really helped.

There are other roadblocks to progress, such as excuses, or stopping when one encounters difficulties, mistakes, or even failures. In the face of these obstacles, you need to either remind yourself of your long-term goal, or you may be called to realign your goals. If you find yourself making excuses, you might go back to chapter 1 to read about how to take on responsibility, starting with your own thoughts and beliefs. Also, resist the temptation to compare yourself to others; each of us walks our own path.

Once you have established your goals and action plan, how important is it to stick to them exactly? You can probably guess the answer: Not so much. The most important thing is that your goals give you direction and movement. Without goals, you would simply drift through life directionless, pushed around by others who would use you to fulfill their dreams.

Another benefit of pursuing goals is the growth you find in the process of accomplishing them. Along the way to your goals, you will learn to overcome obstacles, stay on track, improve yourself, make progress, and celebrate your many achievements. The journey alone will make you happy and fulfilled.

Now, how can you motivate yourself and not procrastinate on your goals? If your vision is strong enough, this will not be a problem. As soon as you feel that nothing is moving forward, first check on your goals. Is your North Star still aligned with your inner compass? Do your mid-term goals still make sense to you? If yes, most probably your motivation has gone up by just thinking about it.

Of course, you will learn new things along the way, and this may have an impact on your perspectives and wishes. Hence, stay flexible and open to unexpected opportunities, check your goals at least monthly, and potentially adapt them from time to time. Revisiting your goals this way is a valuable exercise.

In any case, do not forget to celebrate your achievements along the way. Feel gratitude for what you have achieved. These small celebrations and moments of thanks will help you stay motivated in the long run.

If you set your goals high, as you should, you will almost inevitably have to push your limits and therefore the limits of your comfort zone. You will achieve extraordinary things, and you will grow personally as a result.

Expanding your comfort zone

Throughout my professional career, I often heard managers in trainings advising their employees to "step out of their comfort zone." Especially at the beginning of my career, I was so often out of my comfort zone that I found hearing this advice rather inappropriate. It did not make sense to me why I should feel even more uncomfortable. I felt that if I tried any harder, it would set me up for failure. Back then, it helped me much more to think about "expanding my comfort zone," which made a large difference for me. With that mindset, I could try out exciting, challenging new things, feeling still excited, but safe enough to proceed. Of course, you are never guaranteed to not fail even within your comfort zone. Taking calculated risks and challenging yourself is part of any learning. I would rather call it the "learning zone" instead of the "discomfort zone."

In moments of discomfort, for instance, the five minutes before walking onstage before a large audience, I told myself that afterwards, it will feel good. That thought put me at ease right away. Again, no need to feel unwell, but only excited.

SPEAKING YOUR MIND

Many years ago, when I started a new job and was still learning the complex business of the company, I found myself a member of an important committee. However, I would sometimes hesitate to voice my opinion because I was not sure about it. My manager at the time gave me the feedback that I should step out of my comfort zone and speak my opinion loud and clear. Of course, I did not feel safe stepping out of my comfort zone. Fortunately, I already knew about the power of thoughts and how to foster positive beliefs. Therefore, every morning I told myself, "My opinion is important," and miraculously, without any negative stress or undue feelings, I began to provide my opinion in the committee meetings automatically and comfortably.

In my view, you do not need to dive out of your comfort zone as a way of testing yourself or forcing growth. Rather, you can feel challenged and excited to expand your comfort zone, not anxious or badly stressed. Enlarging your comfort zone will make you grow and reach your ambitious goals.

The perception about us

Coming back to the important point of self-positioning or your personal branding—which essentially just means living by your values—the following is important to realize: If you do not radiate your personal values, others will not recognize who you are, and they will interpret you as something you might not agree with. Also, if you are not clear on who you are, or if you do not live by your values, others find you unpredictable and you might feel insecure yourself.

By no means is it selfish or egoistic to have deeper thoughts about ourselves and who we would like to be. Understanding ourselves and the people around us eases our relationships to others and allows us to live together as a society.

You might think personal branding is probably something only famous people like actors, pop stars, or chief executives of large companies need to do. In my view, there is no need to exaggerate your image, but giving some conscious thought to how you want to be perceived by others is definitely worthwhile. What are your values? What are your strengths? What makes you unique? How do you want to be seen? What do you want to be known for? What is your trademark? Maybe you are and would like to be seen as exceptionally reliable, very knowledgeable, particularly innovative, agile, motivating, caring, respectful, or any number of other things. Besides introspection, a good way to find out how you come across to others is to ask a friendly coworker. Other people, especially conscientious ones, can often describe us very well, if not better, as they can be less subjective.

Whenever you live by your values, you radiate them, and others will notice. With that, you steer others' perception of you. Showing your values elevates your credibility and differentiates you from others. It may even advance your career or increase your circle of influence. This kind of self-awareness is an important part of life mastery.

Another aspect of personal branding is physical and virtual visibility, for instance on social media. Towards the end of this chapter, you will read more about how to make yourself physically visible and heard. So let us consider here your social media presence. It might be worth taking a look at what you can find about yourself on social media. Does your online image show what you really stand for? Is it something you are proud of? Does it highlight your best qualities? If not, and you enjoy being active on social media, you should take action and either remove posts or create new ones that fit your personality. It goes without saying that this is not a one-time exercise, but can become an ongoing process.

Please keep in mind that keeping up an image of something you are genuinely not costs you a lot of energy and will not bring you happiness. However, if you wish to have some qualities you do not yet have, there is nothing wrong with working on them to make them second nature at first and true nature over time. After all, remember: Think positively and highly of yourself!

Let me close this section with explaining the quote in the beginning about the need to design your own life plan. The earlier you understand this the better: In the beginning of your career, you will have managers and mentors who will look after you and will help you advance in your career. They have great things in mind for you because if they train you well, they will get back from you good work results. After some years, once you are well trained and probably have been promoted a few times, you will not so easily find mentors and sponsors anymore. Probably, you became your managers' competition. Then, your managers might even try to keep you small and busy on the team as long as they can reap the great value of your work.

At this point, I hope you understand that you need to become a leader for yourself, the earlier the better. This is not a call against exchanging ideas with your manager or others, but you need to be in the driver's seat of your own life.

BECOMING A LEADER OF YOURSELF

I once interviewed a candidate who was literally hidden by her manager because she was doing such a great job helping him to achieve his own goals. Whenever she wanted to talk about her progress and career, he would delay, saying it was much too early in her development to consider a change. And then from time to time, he would offer her a standard development course that really did not do much for her. After some years, she realized that he did not have much in mind for her other than to keep her doing the tremendous amount of work she was doing for him every day. After she finally realized this, she looked for a position where she could advance and grow outside of his shadow.

Summary

- You can shape your own life by mastering your thoughts, emotions, and activities.

- Shaping activities means aligning them to goals.

- Goal setting consists of two parts: A long-term vision for the next 5 to 10 years and a mid-term goal for the next 12 to 18 months.

- A long-term vision can be seen as your personal North Star, your guiding light to keep you on track over several years. Mid-term goals can be broken down into tangible actions. They give you direction for all the little decisions that must be made every day, consciously or unconsciously.

- Goals ideally should be written down. They need to be positively visualized, slightly exaggerated yet still achievable, and hence measurable, and should give you a great feeling of excitement.

- In order to achieve high goals, you need to grow beyond who you are today. Enlarging your comfort zone is a safe way to seek growth.

- Your personal brand is important, as it makes it easy for others to see your best self and who you really are.

Exercises

1. Think about your long- and mid-term goals and write them down. Remember, your goals need to be positively formulated, and if you can make them visual, even better. Also, make them big—reach for the stars. The more excited you are about your goals, the easier it will be to achieve them.

   Reflect on whether your mid-term goals fully support your long-term goals.

   Accordingly, make plans for each goal in the way described above. Make the first steps particularly easy to reach, such that you can start celebrating your progress soon.

2. What do you stand for? Revisit the section in chapter 2 about knowing your own values. Which ones are particularly interesting for your business life? Which ones make you particularly proud? List at least five values you would like to live and project as your "personal brand." These can be something like timeliness, dependability, professionalism, competence, creativity, diligence, being action-oriented, speed, courtesy, politeness, consideration, respect, kindness, tolerance, and so on.

   For a certain time, ideally at least three weeks, do something each day that is in line with your values. Prepare a table where you label the rows with your selected values and list the dates across the columns. At the end of each day, reflect on the values you have lived out and make a record of them in your table. After a while, you may find patterns. Probably there are values that are easier for you to live, while others take more concerted effort. If you have values that you particularly uphold and that you would like to emphasize further, make a plan on how to live those values.

After three weeks, when the table is filled, reflect on your choice of values. You now have a good sense of what is important to you and what is easier or more difficult to live by. Take the two or three values you like most and make them a part of your personal brand. Doing so with intention will help you to make decisions about how you react to certain situations and where you go from here. Also, whenever you are asked in a job interview about who you are and what values you have, you now have the absolute perfect answer.

3. Think of business leaders, colleagues, as well as people from your private life that you highly appreciate. Write down the characteristics you admire about them. From that list, select those you do not already have on your own values list. Try to live them once in a while. You may even adopt them at a later stage and add them to your own list. This is called personal growth.

Being organized

For every minute spent in organizing, an hour is earned.

—Benjamin Franklin

In order to achieve what we have planned for, we need to manage our time wisely. Strong time management skills not only improve our productivity and let us achieve our goals, but they also reduce stress and the uneasy feeling of underachievement.

The topic of time management could fill a whole book itself, and there are plenty of very good books available. Classics include *The 7 Habits of Highly Effective People* by Stephen R. Covey (1989) and *Getting Things Done: The Art of Stress-Free Productivity* by David Allen (2001). More recent highly praised publications include Cal Newport's *Deep Work: Rules for Focused Success in a Distracted World* (2016) and Nir Eyal's *Indistractable: How to Control Your Attention and Choose Your Life* (2019).

Given the wealth of existing literature on the topic, I only present some highlights that I find important to know. In particular, I want to help you make space for the important parts of your corporate life, allowing you to achieve your goals and ultimately be successful and fulfilled.

In terms of *efficient* time management, having a system is the best way to help you do what you have planned. The exact nature of this system, whether it is a calendar or various to-do lists, may vary depending on the work you are tasked with. For example, if your work is more task- or process-oriented, you may approach it differently than someone who needs to do more people-oriented or strategic work.

Organizing your calendar

An important part of being organized and efficiently using your time is keeping a clear calendar. Ideally, you have only one calendar where you put everything you are planning and working on, not only business but also private events. That way, you have an overview of your entire day. You should also block time in your calendar for less structured activities you want to do, such as strategic thinking or spending time with your partner. This way, you make sure that you have enough time outside of work for healthy relationships, and most importantly for yourself, for example, for exercise, rest, learning, meditation, or whatever is important to you. This will help you keep your workload at a reasonable level, and you will not be tempted to work late into the night, neglecting your most important relationships with yourself and your family and friends. Using time blocks in your calendar will lead to a more sustainable life.

During the day, especially if your calendar is usually full of business meetings, make sure that you have scheduled in personal time. In your work time, you should allow at least half an hour to an hour each day for your own thinking, planning, and strategizing, and the same amount of time for emergencies that you cannot anticipate but still need to handle. Also, it makes sense to reserve a specific time for responding to emails or checking any other collaboration tool so that you do not have to do that all the time, or even worse, after you wanted to leave work for the day.

If you receive a meeting request and your schedule is already full, unless it is an emergency, do not sacrifice your thinking-time slots, but just book the meeting further into the future. This is easier said than done, but it is surely worth trying. In any case, consider first whether the meeting is actually needed and whether it can wait. Otherwise, if too much of your time is taken up by others, you end up not advancing on your own goals and you risk not achieving what really matters to you.

In general, do not commit to more than you can handle. If you repeatedly overcommit yourself, it not only stresses you out and makes you work overtime, but more importantly, chances are high that you cannot deliver what you promised. This will make you known as an unreliable person. In addition, people might stop believing what you say, and you might not get the best opportunities going forward. Frequently falling through on commitments comes from overestimating the time you have available and from wanting to please others. In case you feel pressured to take something on, ask for a day to think about the commitment and check your calendar. In case you often overcommit and struggle to say no, consider that this may come from low self-esteem, as explained in the second section of chapter 1. You might want to revisit that section, as well as the exercises in the last section in chapter 2.

On the other hand, keeping your promises greatly increases your reliability and the trust people have in you. In cases where you have promised to do something and you realize you cannot keep the commitment, make sure you proactively communicate to avoid surprises down the line. This is important for work to be completed by a given deadline but also applies when you are running late to a meeting. You may want to call ahead to let people know. Lateness or failure to keep commitments is interpreted by the other party as a sign of disrespect, as if you were saying, "My time is more valuable than your time." Being reliable generally increases your self-confidence and integrity.

One especially useful tool for efficiency is something I learned in a

LinkedIn Learning course from Chris Croft, one of the UK's leading management trainers. He calls it the "unbroken chain." It is a method of planning in which you write down your promises as well as promises that are made to you in your calendar. Hence, you have an overview on what you promised and who promised you something. When other people have not delivered on their promises, you can remind them in a timely manner. And when they send what they promised to you on time, do not forget to thank them. This way, chances are high that next time they will deliver timely work without needing the reminder. But more importantly, if you note your promises in your calendar, you will not forget them. And if you deliver on your commitments, you will have people's trust.

Creating lists wisely

Now that you have your calendar organized in time blocks, you need to decide on what exactly you want to do within a block. For some blocks, it will be straightforward or scheduled events will be given to you, but especially for those where you want to get work done, you need to do some further planning. The simplest way to do this is with lists you either keep in your calendar, your mobile phone or, as I do, on a sheet of paper in front of you. To avoid being overwhelmed by the myriad tasks you want or need to accomplish, keep at least two lists. One is a short daily list; the other is sort of a master list going out longer. The daily list you either craft in the morning or, if you are really organized, as the last thing of your business day. This way, you have an overview of what you need and promised to do that day. The nice thing about writing this list at the end of your workday is that you do not have to worry about whether you have anything left to do; everything moves to tomorrow's plan. With that, you can have a more relaxed evening and night. And each day, you write a new list. This small list of a handful of to-dos helps you to have a feeling of control and focus.

In some management literature, to-do lists are dismissed as ineffective because they either paralyze you or tempt you to prioritize shorter and easier tasks and neglect longer ones. In fact, they easily can be counterproductive if applied in an adverse way. In my view, the overall goal is to organize yourself and be clear on what you want to do. Writing something down typically brings clarity. If you are aware of potential pitfalls, you can turn your lists into a useful instrument. First, your daily list needs to be short. It goes without saying that you have already sorted out what is neither urgent nor important for you to do, and that you have delegated what is urgent but unimportant, if possible. Also, do not put things on your list that you already know you will not do. One of my favorite quotes from the management expert Peter Drucker is the following: "There is nothing so useless as doing efficiently that which should not be done at all."

At the beginning of your workday, determine what is most important to do, and in what order you should do it. Obviously, the urgent and important things should go first. To avoid procrastination, it helps to tackle the most unpleasant or toughest task first thing in the morning instead of putting it off until later. The success of getting it done and the feeling of accomplishment will motivate you for the rest of the day. Rather than putting off tough or unpleasant tasks and letting them torture you all day long while you get nothing else done, complete the toughest task or the task you dislike most to free you up for constructive thoughts and work you like. Just to be clear, you should start your day with a prioritized list; otherwise, you tend to work on urgent easy tasks, but not on the most important ones.

The other type of list is sort of a master list where you note your tasks and goals that go well beyond this or the next day. It can contain things you want to do in areas outside of work, like your home, your finances, your family, your health, your holidays, and so on. Some entries you will then transfer to your daily list. Ideally, every day you would pull an entry from the master list to your daily list, but this may not always be practical. This master list can be a rather fuzzy one. There will be things on this list that maybe you will never do. This list is more a container to store your thoughts and to take inspiration from, and you do not have to feel bad if you are not achieving what is on it by the end of each day.

There are enviable people who have this all in their head or who have a supreme intuition that always tells them what to do next. They do not need written lists. All other people, however, need to somehow write down their priority tasks if they want to get important things done.

Sometimes people complain about having to structure their day. They want to have the freedom to run over during meetings, have a longer coffee break, or do something completely different than they had planned. In principle, there is nothing wrong with being flexible occasionally. However, you need to be aware that repeatedly allowing this kind of flexibility may take away time from other important areas of your life, such as time with friends or family. You must personally weigh what is more important to you.

Please do not underestimate what your lists do for you. If you do not have them, you may be spending your time working on things that are most important to other people, but not necessarily to you. Or you may be spending too much time on unimportant things that come up during the day without advancing on your true goals. Just remember, achievement and progress will give you contentment.

Ways out of procrastination

Having everything well organized, your goals written up and action plans established, why do so many of us still not advance on our life goals? I see three reasons: perfectionism, procrastination, and distraction. If we want to do things too perfectly, we often plan for too long, then delay the completion of our tasks and get less done in the end. Analytical people are especially prone to this. As Voltaire said, "Perfect is the enemy of good." Procrastination, though, makes us not even start or causes us to advance hesitantly on a task. It makes us put off tasks and events, reschedule constantly, and avoid things, although they are important to us. Finally, distractions are actions other than those intended that keep us from completing our task and ultimately achieving our goals. All three can be equally destructive to our plans and goals.

Procrastination is complex and can have several causes. For instance, you might put something off for *fear of failure*, where you actually fear that your efforts will fall short, and because you worry that you cannot meet your own high standards, you do not start at all. By becoming aware of these reasons and then consciously thinking about how to positively shape your thoughts and beliefs about the tasks, you can take control of your tendencies toward procrastination and perfectionism. If you build confidence to move and take opportunities, you will advance.

Another frequent reason for procrastination is a *lack of focus*. If you do not have any goals set, most probably you lack focus, as you have no target to work towards. The more inspirational and purposeful yet attainable goals you have, the more you will be able to advance in a direction rather than drifting through life. Also, if you have a strong purpose for getting things done, you will surely complete the tasks. I have never seen people more efficient in the workplace than parents with young children. Some did not work 100 percent, but maybe 70–80 percent, and they tended to get more done than their peers who did a 100 percent job. They knew exactly how much time they had per day because they had to pick up their children at a specific time, no matter what. Because they had no flexibility whatsoever after a certain hour of the day, they planned their days very well, but also knew when a work product was good enough to release. Additionally, they were impressively concentrated during their day.

Similar to lacking focus is when you have so much on your to-do list that you do not even know where to start. With the help of daily lists that are prioritized, you can point your attention at one item.

The biggest and probably most common, though underestimated reason for procrastination in my view is people lacking the energy to devote to a task. Having low energy levels prevents you from taking action and moving forward. So, people are waiting for motivation. But motivation will not come by waiting; it only comes by doing. I will come back to this important topic later in this section.

In any case, the more you know about why you procrastinate, the more you can do about it. Regardless of the cause, you could also try the following:

- Allocate time in your calendar for the task.

- Have an action plan with several steps. The more difficulty you have advancing in a task, the more you should break it down into discrete steps that you can plan. Taking small steps in the beginning will let you achieve something fast, and that will motivate you to take next steps.

- Set reasonable deadlines for each of your tasks. It tends to be that the time you set for something is the minimum time you will use. I often tell myself, if I give something unlimited time, it will take forever. Hence, setting a deadline in advance helps to keep you moving at a good pace.

- Once you have started, make sure you do not get distracted. I will come to this further down.

- Reward yourself after completing each step. This does not need to be anything big. It could be as simple as quietly praising yourself, taking a short break, getting coffee with a colleague, up to going for a walk, rewarding yourself with an evening out, or watching a movie to relax. The important thing is to fully savor your rewards, not merging them in with the next task already. Small celebrations leave you with a good feeling of accomplishment and success. By the way, if you reward yourself in this way, you will be more likely to start tasks and more efficient and focused while performing them. Additionally, you have built in breaks to prevent yourself from getting exhausted and overworked.

- Tell one or several people that you will be doing the task, such that you build a bit of healthy social pressure. Do not tell it to everyone, though, because doing that may cause you to already feel too good about their anticipatory reactions and not take the necessary steps to begin or move forward.

- Visualize how great you will feel once you have finished the task and how bad you will feel if you do not finish it. Think about the downside of putting the task off and what the consequences will be.

- Finally, remember from chapter 1, that what you think about makes all the difference. If you think a task will be cumbersome, doing it will most probably feel that way. If you say you have no time, time will seem to slip away. On the other hand, if you think you will make good progress and everything will run smoothly, and if you say that you have sufficient time available, you most probably will work in flow, and it will feel like you complete the task in no time.

Antidote for distractions

While procrastination has to do with hesitation, distractions, in my view, are a whole other story. Distractions actively pull us away from what we initially intended to do. We do not hesitate over doing our task, we just simply do something else altogether. It could be chatting with a coworker who came by our desk, checking emails when a pop-up notification pings, scrolling through social media feeds, or watching television when we actually planned to do something else. And distractions can get you hooked, like when you find yourself endlessly scrolling through social media feeds or hooked on computer games. Distractions abound, but typically there is a root cause to why we let ourselves be distracted.

RECOGNIZING OVERLOAD

Whenever I was going through a very stressful period of time—maybe I had a lot on my plate at work, difficult decisions to make, typically coupled with some unsolved issues with the family—I frequently did a Sudoku on my way home, during lunchtime, or even in the evening. Solving this logic-based number puzzle needed my full attention, and it gave me a few minutes of full control and achievement. That was the only reason, I guess, why I was doing it. In normal times, I would consider this as a complete waste of an hour. Once I realized that for me solving Sudokus was a sign of overload, I started to look for root causes of my stress and what I could do to counter them instead of distracting myself with something else. Most of the time, I found the root causes rather quickly, but fully solving them was obviously not always as quick and easy as solving a Sudoku. However, a lot of positive thinking, combined with clear affirmations and visualizing a time when things would be better, worked very powerfully and soon relaxed the situation.

In my view, we are more likely to let ourselves be distracted if we feel emotionally uncomfortable. Hence, starting with addressing our inner state is the most promising way to stay focused. But first, we need to become aware that we are distracted, as the signs of that sometimes can be rather subtle. And even before that, the prerequisite is to know what we actually set out to do, in order to know what we were distracted from. Having a tidy calendar broken down into time blocks, as explained above, may help you to become aware of how you intended to spend your time. This will give you the chance to go against what has distracted you so far and refocus on the things you really wanted to do. With this awareness, you will be able to achieve the goals you have set for yourself, which will give you a sense of purpose and will increase your happiness and contentment.

Now, getting free of distractions is sometimes not that easy. On the one hand, there may be distractions you produce yourself, like constantly checking emails and social media, or your mind wandering away from what you decided to focus on. Then there may be external distractions, like phone calls or colleagues coming by your office desk. These types of distractions oftentimes are not very productive, and it is good to preempt them during periods you had set aside for doing certain work. You could block times in your shared calendar so other people know when you do or do not have time for a chat or question, or when you respond to email. You should also block out times when your coworkers can see that you do not want to be distracted. Nir Eyal in his book *Indistractable* (2019) gives detailed solutions on what one can do to counter the various sources of distractions. He also advises: "Think of all the ways people steal your time…If we don't plan our days, someone else will."

Getting free of distractions is particularly important if your work involves activities that need your full concentration and push your cognitive capabilities to their limit. It is this type of highly valuable work that creates new insights and brings companies forward. This type of work requires your full, uninterrupted focus. Typically, such activities bring you into flow, where you work in a state of complete immersion. The only thing worse than getting distracted once you are in flow is never getting into flow at all because of all the distractions. Interruptions during such type of work can be frustrating, and they can also lead to mistakes. Cal Newport's bestselling book *Deep*

Work (2016) tells us about how to not get distracted from such types of work. He describes several rules for facilitating performance at the highest level. Those include training your mind to be concentrated, focused, and attentive; wisely deciding which social media to participate in; and cutting out work that does not need to be done at all. He claims that you cannot do more than four hours a day of "deep" work, hence in a workday, there is ample time left to do "shallow" work like replying to emails, participating in meetings, writing reports—activities that require less concentrated focus.

In any case, it is a good thing to block out times in your calendar when you need to focus alone versus times when you can communicate with others and complete less demanding tasks. Keep in mind that time management is for you to be productive, performing, and progressing and still to have enough time for the things and people that really matter to you.

Energy management is more important than time management

Let me go back to what I noted earlier about low energy being a major cause of procrastination. In my opinion, energy management is more important than time management, especially in the longer term. If you regularly use more energy than you can regenerate, you will fall ill or burn out, your body's way of forcing you to recharge. Depending on how badly you overwork yourself, burnout can happen in a rather short span of several months, or it can take years to decades. The symptoms may not go as far as severe illness, but typical signs of low energy include not feeling joy or excitement anymore. If you find that nothing gives you pleasure anymore, not your family, not your house, not nice vacations, not your sports car, then it is high time to do some serious energy management. Better, of course, is to do good energy management on a daily basis, before burnout hits.

The German medical doctor Ulrich Bauhofer explains it as follows: "Energy is like money. If you permanently spend more than you earn, you will be broke in the foreseeable future: Energetically insolvent. Therefore, make sure you have a balanced energy budget." He also claims, "The way we work doesn't work. Almost one in three has high blood pressure, 58 percent of managers are overweight and 56 percent have questionable cholesterol levels" (Bauhofer 2020). Whatever the exact percentages are in your part of the world, the fact is that too many people these days are stressed to the point of negatively affecting their health.

What gives and takes energy for each of us can be somewhat personal. However, the following are typical energy takers everyone is exposed to:

- Lack of rest: Taking frequent enough breaks and resting, including getting good sleep, helps us to cope with the tremendous amount of information that comes at us every day. Far too many people in corporations do not get enough rest. They even pride themselves for not needing long hours of sleep. However, this results in stress and lower productivity.

  We all know that sleep is important. While we sleep, not only does the brain reorganize information, but it also regenerates physically. Tiredness accumulates. Studies have shown that when we are not sleeping enough, our ability to concentrate decreases dramatically, as does our ability to make decisions. Most of all, our zest for life decreases. Dr. Bauhofer claims, "If you are not rested, then the greatest fireworks can go off, it will not touch you and you will not be able to enjoy it. If you are rested on the other hand, you can enjoy very simple things, the song of a bird, a sun beam or a rainy day."

  The more you are stressed, the more important it is to take breaks. With the energy you gain, you will advance faster and be more relaxed afterwards.

- Lack of exercise: In the corporate world, it is easy to get caught in a vicious cycle of inactivity, declining fitness, and fatigue. If you feel you cannot make time for exercise or regular walks, just recall the saying of another German medical doctor, Sebastian Kneipp: "If you do not have time for your health every day, you will need a lot of time for your illnesses later on." We all know that health is our highest priority. It is the basis for all other areas of life. Without a certain degree of health, everything is nothing.

- Lack of light and fresh air: The only root source of energy we have on our planet is the sun. Hence, it should come as no surprise that you can get energy from going outside in the sun. Also, our cells need oxygen to produce the energy the body needs. So going outside after your lunch break is an easy way to boost your energy level for a productive afternoon.

- Lack of time for introspection: Every person needs to find a balance between looking outward and looking inward. Always facing outward may cause us to be disconnected from our inner self and we may do things that are beyond our strength. Hence, introspection helps us to respect our limits. It also helps us understand ourselves and others, and contributes to emotional and physical health.

Whereas the above items are very basic energy takers, the following are energy takers that can often be found in our work environment:

- Stress: Stressors in one's work include needing to work under time pressure, responsibilities we cannot cope with, and strong competition, but also tasks that underchallenge us, conflicts between personal and professional goals, and mental exhaustion. Whereas a little bit of stress can be energizing, constant or large stress can drastically lower your energy level. Becoming aware of stress and its root causes is the start for better dealing with it.

- Overstrain and overwork: Both go along with overutilizing your own energy and can cause serious stress, exhaustion, and other health disorders. Next to overexploitation of mental resources, not having enough rest, and bad time management, in the severe cases I saw in my career, overstrain had more to do with unhelpful underlying beliefs. People believed they were not performing well enough in their jobs, and they were therefore reluctant to ask for help. If this is the case, you should work on the beliefs you have about yourself. In the last section of this chapter, you can read about how to do this and what other benefits you will get from it.

- Lack of purpose: An incredible energy thief is thinking you are doing useless work. It makes you feel bored or even desperate. If you find purpose in the activity you are doing, it is easier to get into flow and enjoy doing the work you are supposed to do, and your energy will be filled by feeling deep joy.

- Job dissatisfaction: If you are either seriously over- or underchallenged in your job, do not like what you do, see no growth opportunities anymore, have difficulties with your manager, or are dissatisfied with your job in any number of other ways, you experience stress in the form of either anxiety or boredom. Whatever the case, addressing the dissatisfaction will recover your energy level.

- Lack of appreciation and recognition: Some will say that they are strong enough not to need external recognition for a job well done. However, if your work is not appreciated, your presence is taken for granted, or your efforts are not valued, then you pretty quickly get demotivated. Studies show that the satisfaction of getting paid more money is only temporary and lasts, on average, two weeks. But honest appreciation has a totally different power. The easiest form of appreciation and celebration is to say, "Thank you for your work." It will make people feel appreciated and energized, and what you give will be reflected back to you.

The following are energy takers that I experienced quite often at work. However, they can also come from your private life:

- Inner emotional conflicts and chronic worries: Nothing steals as much energy from you as opposing inner thoughts and beliefs, or a constant negative inner voice. Also, frequent worrying about the future or pondering over the past can take over your thoughts such that you have difficulty concentrating and doing what you actually want to do.

- Energy vampires: This is what I call people who take our energy by simply being around us. I am sure you have encountered people like this before. You talk to someone for a while and when they leave, you feel depleted. It may be that these people only talk about themselves, or they dump their problems and worries on us, or they give unsolicited advice. It also can be that they make us feel like we are doing something wrong. In one way or another, their way of talking completely takes us over and after such talks, we feel exhausted, while the other person asks us when we can chat again, as they gained energy from our talk, taking it from our own energy reserves.

What really helps is simply not spending time with people who stress us out or irritate us. However, it could be that the energy vampire is your manager or a relative or someone else you are frequently exposed to and cannot avoid. In such cases, you should find means to shorten the conversation or, once you are aware of their tendencies, adopt a mindset such that nothing this person says really gets to you and their words simply roll off you instead.

Just keep in mind that energy vampires do not tap into the energy of others on purpose. They oftentimes just talk to others this way to compensate for their own weakness and insecurity.

- Negative conversations or naysayers: Similar to energy vampires, people who are chronically pessimistic, who see problems all over and only have negative conversations with other people, are lowering the energy balance of everyone involved, including themselves. People who constantly complain about everything and everyone are a great burden to others. Here again, you need to become aware of the problematic behavior and actively address it, by only engaging in the discussion as far as needed.

Now, in our daily lives, it is almost impossible to have all these energy takers under control all the time. For instance, we might be stressed about completing a project and doing challenging work under time pressure. Obviously, we can do this for a limited period of time, and if we care for ourselves well during this time, for instance by taking breaks to get fresh air, eating high-quality food, and getting enough sleep, we might even be able to sustain this stress for a certain time. But we should not fool ourselves. Utilizing more energy than we can regenerate is not sustainable over a longer period of time. As said before, this period can be several years, in which you slowly but surely lower your energy account. Even if you are able to function for a prolonged period with chronically low energy levels, it may well be that some external event, such as a new manager whose ideas do not align with yours or a failure in a project, will bring you to your knees.

GUARDING AGAINST BURNOUT

In my corporate career, I have seen several top managers who unfortunately burned out. In the end, it was probably always the combination of two things: First, their energy account was diminished after many years of ambitiously building their careers and trying to survive in top management. Second, they suddenly encountered difficulties in their environment, such as a new colleague or a new manager who attacked them and who did not support them. Unable to cope with a new stressor while their energy levels were already chronically low, they unfortunately had to quit their jobs to recover and regain their strength and energy.

Whether you are a top manager or not, as a rule of thumb, the more demanding your job becomes, the more closely you have to monitor your energy in order to stay resilient.

Energy givers

When you see people who have mastered this energy game—that is, people who know how to recharge, and who knowingly or unknowingly do exactly the right things to avoid depleting their energy—you will notice that they seem amazingly youthful and dynamic, even if they are of retirement age. Typically, these individuals even work many years longer than others and have particular creative power.

Above, I have listed energy takers and how to avoid them, as well as the respective energy givers. Here are some further energy givers not yet mentioned:

- Belonging: You probably experienced before that when you do something together with a group and belonging to this group, everything goes much easier. When you are accepted by the group and share the same visions and goals, you are more motivated to help others, which in turn makes you happier. Work is more fun, and achievements bring more joy. On the other hand, if you feel that you do not belong to the group you are working with, you will not be able to give your full performance and it will cost you a lot of energy to do your tasks.

  We spend too much time at work to feel like we belong only in our personal lives. Finding a company, a department, a group, a workplace in which you feel you belong is vitally important for your energy, happiness, and health.

- Spending time with family and friends: Nothing can be more inspiring than being together with good friends or family, experiencing activities together, listening and being heard, exchanging ideas, feeling affection, having joyful experiences. It enriches our lives, and we become more cheerful, fulfilled, and energized.

- Spending time in nature: Besides the health effects of light, fresh air, and exercise, spending time in nature helps us to connect with the source. This brings you closer to yourself and who you really are. To immerse yourself in nature and experience its full effects, switch off or disconnect all electronics. Then you will better notice the abundance in nature; let it give you new insights and inspire your creativity. Afterward, you will come back from nature less stressed, with a calmer mind and a broader perspective.

- Meditation: The most direct way to experience inner stillness, lasting well-being, and increased energy is meditation. Studies show that meditation increases your physical, mental, and emotional health, and increases your resilience as well. You become more capable of handling setbacks. It extends your attention span and enhances your self-awareness, which may trigger positive changes in your life. As a side effect, it also increases your productivity and creativity. It has been shown that meditation gives you deeper rest even than sleep. In any case, meditation connects you to your inner self and brings you closer to what truly matters in your life. You more easily gain clarity about what you want and what you do not want in life. You feel more balanced, more confident, more empathetic, more purposeful, more positive, and more energetic. When selecting a meditation technique, it makes sense to learn a solid technique that has a long tradition. Otherwise, you may risk mental instability.

For me, a daily meditation practice has incredible power for helping me find balance and getting many things done in a calm way. I truly believe that I could not have managed my professional and personal life as well without meditation.

- Enjoying a variety of activities: A varied portfolio of activities you love to do can favorably balance your energy level. It is highly unlikely that every single activity will use your energy to the same extent, and quite likely that some will give you a lot of energy. Typically, people report feeling totally refreshed after a painting lesson, a choir rehearsal, or a long-distance run. For me, spending two hours in an orchestra rehearsal has always felt like a miracle in terms of boosting my energy level.

- Feeling thankfulness: Nothing contributes more to contentment than thankfulness. The good news is that contentment and gratitude can be learned by a very simple technique. Just note down three things you are grateful for every day before you go to sleep. Your level of contentment will raise dramatically. As the Roman scholar Marcus Cicero stated, "Gratitude is not only the greatest of virtues, but the parent of all others."

- Finding joy in life: If there is one simple expression of life's energy, then it is the expression of joy in laughter and smiles. Children laugh about 400 times a day, whereas adults laugh on average twenty times a day. This is a sign of how life energy diminishes over the years. Hence, spending time with children can be very uplifting.

The less you feel you have to laugh about, the more you should search for positive things in your life and seek out beautiful and enjoyable moments to celebrate.

Whenever you feel joy and excitement, you can be sure that you are on the right track. Take them as your guiding principles and you will walk the optimal path for you.

In summary, if your energy account is running low, your decision-making ability, your ability to concentrate, your efficiency, your memory and zest for life dramatically shrink. To keep your life in balance, you need to keep your energy in balance. Resilience, the agility of our mind, the ability to remain positive, innovative, and flexible even under difficult circumstances, all correlate directly with your energy level and are important to maintain, especially in times of crisis. Remaining mindful of the demands you make yourself is the start. If you fill your schedule, seriously consider whether you can energetically do all that you set out to accomplish in a day. We all have limited time and energy, so whenever you add something new to your life, think at the same time about dropping things that no longer serve you. Seriously consider managing your energy with the same diligence as your time.

Energy management is an important step towards life mastery. When it comes to your time and your energy, no one is responsible for your life and your happiness except yourself.

Summary

- Being organized is the first step to getting done the things we would like to do.

- A good method for organizing our day is blocking time for activities we would like to do, privately as well as for our work. For our business day, very short daily lists help us to complete each day's tasks. It's best to prioritize the list and start with the toughest task first, as achieving it gives motivation for the rest of the day.

- The daily list is fed by short-term assignments and items from a master list which contains things we would like to do over a longer horizon. Having things written down in lists keeps our mind free and not preoccupied worrying about whether we might have missed anything.

- Perfectionism, procrastination, and distractions prevent us from reaching our goals. There are several ways to beat them; however, it starts with becoming aware of what it is that is holding you back.

- In the long run, managing our energy is even more important than managing our time. Simple things like getting enough sleep, fresh air, sunlight, and eating nutritious food can boost your energy. In the work environment, low energy levels come from stress, overwork, lack of purpose, job dissatisfaction, and lack of appreciation and recognition.

Exercises

1. Think about how you have organized your calendar. Have you set time blocks for your private life? If you frequently work overtime, seriously consider blocking out time for your private life.

2. If you are not already using lists to stay organized, try it out for a period of time. First, write down your master list. It will not take long. You could do this in the form of a mind map, with branches like work, partner, family, friends, home, health, vacations, finances, etc. Then, create a daily list for the next day. Be careful not to overload it; assign yourself a handful of tasks, but not too many more. Use your intuition to create and prioritize your to-dos. Keep this up for at least a full work week. At the end of each day, or when writing the next daily list, reflect on how the list helped you accomplish what you wanted to do. Also, think about what did not go according to plan and why. The more you know about why you are putting something off, the better you can do

something about it the next day. At the end of the week, reflect on this exercise and decide how you want to work with lists in the future.

3. If you struggle with tasks you dislike doing, do the following for an entire work week: Work through the task you like least first thing in the morning. Be very rigorous about it and do not skip a day without doing this. After having completed the task, and also at the end of each day, reflect on how you feel about it and whether you want to continue with this technique. You might just find this way of working will raise your success greatly and maybe even change your life.

4. Reflect on the social media tools you are utilizing. Do they contribute to using your time wisely? Do they help you to get things done? Do you enjoy using them? If yes, no problem. If no, set them aside. If you are unsure, try to live a month without checking them. You do not need to uninstall them, or tell anyone about your social media sabbatical in advance. Just see what happens and after a month's time, check whether you really missed out on things. Would the last month have been much better with this social media tool? Did anyone care that you were not using the tool? If your answers are both "no," then consider now going back and uninstalling the tool. Logging off social media will give you back precious time that you can now use for things you really care about.

5. Reflect on what consumes your energy: Which activities cost you a lot of energy, and which seem almost effortless for you? How draining or invigorating are your relationships with colleagues, employees, or superiors? Are you able to develop freely? Do you have a sufficient sense of achievement? Do you feel a sense of purpose in your work? Do you enjoy sufficient recognition in your professional and private life? How well can you "switch off" after work? How energetic do you feel after a vacation or a weekend? Can you quickly rebalance your energy after a stressful situation?

    If you want to do something for your energy balance, choose one or two of the energy givers described above and implement them in your life. Do not choose too many at once, because chances are that you will not be able to keep up with all of them. Just keep in mind that sometimes even small things can have a big impact if you engage in them steadily.

On self-development

Anyone who stops learning is old, whether at 20 or 80. Anyone who keeps learning stays young. The greatest thing in life is to keep your mind young.
—Henry Ford

Self-development has become an incredible trend. Everyone talks about learning and development, you can find tons of articles about it, top management is talking about it, consultants are promoting it . . . but it still remains somewhat unclear what you should learn and develop. Whereas learning is taking knowledge from books, courses, teachers, or other people, development goes beyond that. It is the process that starts after learning. It is about bringing the knowledge into practice, mastering skills, and making them part of our behavior and habits. Going forward, though, I will use the terms rather interchangeably. In this section, I will write about why self-development suddenly became so important, and what types of learners and learning there are. Also, I will write about how to choose what to learn next and how to find the right sources to facilitate learning.

The need for self-development now and in the future

Whether we want to believe it or not, in the past few years, progress has accelerated. The more well-educated people there are working on something, the faster progress and evolution will happen. It is that simple. In fact, there are many industries where such dramatic progress has been made that people have become largely redundant. We are in the middle of a period of change where repetitive work is being taken over by computer systems with the help of artificial intelligence. Whole professions are being made obsolete, but luckily, many new professions are being created as well. Hence, it is of utmost importance, especially for those who are already advanced in their careers, to stay alert and agile with regards to their professional activities. These days, companies are particularly concerned about up-skilling or re-skilling the workforce.

There are also other less threatening and more general reasons for self-development. Remember the lesson evolution dictates: Every living thing on this earth is growing, and if it is not, then it is dying. Not only do our bodies need to constantly grow new cells, but our minds also need to grow, otherwise they will decline. Furthermore, as you read earlier in this book, life is about expanding happiness, and evolution is the process through which this is fulfilled. And evolution requires self-development. For your corporate work life, this means that if your work allows you to *grow and develop*, you will have a particularly satisfying career that makes you particularly happy. Again, progress adds to your happiness.

Learning will also help you reach the high goals you have set for yourself. If your goals are ambitious, then you most probably need to learn new skills or tactics to achieve them. In addition, developing yourself also makes you more confident as a person, whether by investing in your communication skills, developing critical thinking or problems-solving skills, or any other learning you do to improve yourself. Ultimately, self-development will raise your self-awareness and contribute to you feeling fulfilled.

Generally, corporations see learning and development as a competitive advantage for better business performance in terms of productivity and customer satisfaction, and as an employee benefit in attracting and keeping top talent. In fact, one of the big reasons why employees change companies is that they do not see a possibility to grow and move their career forward.

There are several types of learners and several types of learning

Before we can decide on what to learn next, we need to understand how we should approach learning. Some people swear by "learning on the job." Whereas this is probably the fastest and most efficient way in the beginning, not every position stretches you enough to continue your learning over a longer period of time. In such cases, moving to a new position is recommended. However, the longer you are in business, the less likely you will be able to go from one position to the next. Often without realizing it, people who swear by only "learning on the job" become outdated. Hence, they tend to stay at the same jobs even longer, and once they do decide to move on, chances are high that they will not find a position they find adequate for themselves.

Now, for "learning on the job" you initially need to make quite an effort. Say you will work an extra hour a day to learn what is needed. You will most likely continue to put in this extra hour even when you do not learn new things on the job because you simply are used to it and because your manager is used to it too. Hence, you work more, but you may gain nothing from this extra hour for yourself. And the longer you go on like this, the more learning opportunities you are losing out on. This may potentially make you less employable in the future, as it might be that your type of work has declined in importance, for example due to progress in automation. Hence, you realize you have to seek out learning other than "on the job" in order to stay relevant.

There is another type of learner who tries to learn everything about the industry and the field they are in. They read many articles and keep up to date with the latest developments. Typically, this type of learner is also active on social media, and they follow industry news like who moved to which job. This type of learner, however, just learns what most others are learning too. Hence, they will not have a significant advantage above others, and frankly, over a decade, say, being super-informed about people's moves and similar news has no real value. Also, being informed about every industry hype, often steered by consulting companies trying to find new business fields, can be tiring, inefficient, and rather ineffective too.

There is yet another type of learner who is purposefully continuing their education. These learners individually select what they want to master going forward. Typically, they do not try to learn twenty things at a time, but deliberately choose a specific field to focus on. This type of learning requires some foresight and also a general understanding of where the respective industry or field is moving towards. The downside of this type of learning is that you might select an area of focus to the best of your knowledge, only to potentially educate yourself in something that turns out to not really be that relevant in the long run.

In order to be comprehensive, I also need to present to you the last type of learner: the "no learner," who is convinced that he or she already knows how things run. They appreciate that they do not know everything, but they are convinced that they know enough to do what they are supposed to do. Unfortunately, with such an overconfident attitude, you cannot learn, make progress, and get better. These individuals actually present a pretty sad situation, and I have seen it more often in my career than I thought I ever would. Only the realization that there is something to learn creates the basis for successful learning.

So what is the best way of learning? I would say, take a bit of everything. When starting in a new role, it is definitely good to learn as much as possible on the job. Later, the biggest learning effect you can get is by targeting a field or a skill that interests you and that is relevant to the market you are in. And throughout your career, you should try to learn about the most important developments in your industry. This means reading industry articles and informing yourself about important news and developments.

Coming to the different types of learning, traditionally, Human Resources suggests that 70 percent of learning in corporations should be done experimentally "by doing" on the job, 20 percent socially "by observing and interacting" with others, and 10 percent through formal training.

Especially when you are new in a job or a specific field, or if you are tasked with a special project or challenging assignment, "learning by doing" is very efficient. Under these circumstances, you can gain experience quickly. The downside perhaps is that this process may be prone to error. Depending on what you are doing, this may be more or less critical.

"Learning by observing and interacting" can be also very effective. It can be by doing a stint or temporary assignment in another group or department, or through a job rotation where you switch jobs with someone for a few days or more. However, in my career, I have not seen job rotation really work as it was intended. Typically, such programs are difficult to organize. Job shadowing is similar but is much easier to set up. Here, a person follows another person for a day or two and gets insight into that person's business field and working style.

An organized way to learn new tasks is by "task immersion," where you learn from colleagues about one of their tasks and help with the work involved. This learning setup can range from a few hours to a few days spent immersing yourself in this new task, and the situation ensures that you are certainly learning something. I will describe this high-value process further in the last chapter of this book.

Another method which falls into this same category is social learning, or learning from a mentor or coach who shares his or her insights and gives advice. Also, receiving feedback and guidance from others on your performance and work products can lead to good learning.

You can also achieve good learning by watching or listening to speeches and presentations in your company, at conferences, or on the internet. There you not only can learn about a topic, but you can observe how people perform and what works or does not work so well in their presentation styles.

One way of combining technical learning with social learning that a lot of companies have introduced is hosting "lunch and learn" sessions, where employees can learn about topics during their lunch hour at a presentation hosted and catered by the company. I like these rather informal events, which typically take place every month or so, where people are encouraged to learn but also can socialize and openly exchange ideas. It is a great way to fostering a learning culture in corporations.

A more recent way of learning from your peers is via business networks or other social media channels, where subject matter experts nowadays give opinions and share insights that can contribute to your learning.

The challenge of "learning by observing" is to make sure that you learn from the right people. Nothing is as effective as learning from the best. However, as with any sort of source, you need to check the source's credibility to ensure you are getting correct information and good explanations.

Of course, you can always seek out "formal learning" through specifically designed training sessions, like taking classes at the university or from specific learning networks, or participating in training courses offered by your corporation. It also encompasses reading, self-study programs, and any courses or structured e-learning classes. The good thing about picking up skills through formal learning is that you can choose a reputable provider yourself and get access to best-in-class training. Personally, I am a big fan of reading books or reviewed articles to grow my knowledge. However, these days, many resources exist over all sorts of media, like podcasts or short video tutorials.

The agony of choice, or what we should learn and develop

Up-skilling and re-skilling are big issues these days. Up-skilling is when you learn more in your current role, and re-skilling involves learning new skills for a completely different job. In this, and as far as lifelong learning is concerned, the question remains: What should we ideally be learning? My answer is that one should always set out to learn a mixture of general and technical skills.

Whenever you take a step forward in your career, you will need new skills in order to bring value to the next place you will be working. Hence, selecting what to learn is a key component to achieving the goals you have set for yourself. You should not learn something which is absolutely not in line with your goals. This requires, though, knowing what you want. A good way to think about what you should learn is to figure out what activities you enjoy and ask yourself whether you would find joy in further mastering them. For instance, say you enjoy technical analysis. You would first give it more attention by practicing it on the job. Every time you have to do an analysis, go an extra mile and explore how you might enhance it. Then exchange deeper thoughts about it with peers and probably even do some further study on the subject by taking an e-learning course or reading a book on the topic.

Joy and excitement are always good measures of whether something is right for you. If you feel neither joy nor purpose in learning a new skill, you may struggle to learn it, and chances are that you will not complete what you intended to learn. Sometimes, though, you need to learn something to overcome a hurdle that is keeping you from further expanding. In this case, you might not feel too much joy in the beginning, but you have a strong purpose to learn it. Once you mastered the new skill, you might feel joy, but in this case, it only comes afterwards. However, it will be very satisfying, as you will experience growth.

The training industry, especially e-platforms, has dramatically grown in the past years. It has become easier than ever to get high-quality training at a low price or even for free. Outstanding sites like Coursera or edX let you take courses from top-ranked universities and industry-leading companies. Another resource is LinkedIn Learning, which hosts courses by industry experts. As fantastic as these resources are, it has also become much harder to find one's way among all the options and sort out the great courses from the mediocre or time-wasting ones. In this sense, attending a traditional course can be a surer route, as it will be more interactive and will therefore allow you to ask individual questions.

TWO WAYS TO ADVANCE

In my corporate career, when I was asked to give advice to people in finance or risk departments on what they could do to progress in their own careers, I often found two promising ways to go. One way was by furthering their technical skills pertaining to data—interpreting it, analyzing it, visualizing it, classifying it, and so on. This area of learning is about acquiring technical skills so you can perform analyses yourself, rather than being dependent on other people to process the data before you can do anything with it.

The second area of growth is in strengthening general skills like communication. You can be a top expert and have outstanding technical skills, but if you cannot communicate your findings to a larger audience, to management, or to non-experts in your field, you will always be dependent on other people to do this for you: Influencing others will be harder, and you will likely face misunderstanding or frustration. I have never seen anyone fail who honestly tried to improve their communication skills. In fact, I observed significant progress in those who focused on this area. Another piece of advice I like to give is: develop some leadership skills, regardless of whether you are formally in a leadership position. I consider everyone to be a leader of someone, starting with yourself.

Most companies work with mandatory personal development plans, which provide a good structure for learning. If your manager is really interested in your progress, they will help you craft a personal development plan, and even if they do not, it is worthwhile to have your own personal development plan in writing. In there, note what things you have to learn in order to advance towards your goals. Ideally, you will be eager to learn about a mix of things based on your current strengths and weaknesses. With that, you can improve yourself and your skills, your work will become even more valuable to your company, and your personal satisfaction and compensation will rise.

Many times, I have been asked whether it is necessary to earn further professional qualifications, such as certifications or diplomas. My view is that it really depends on what area you are working in and, to a lesser extent, what type of person you are. There are some professions, like actuaries or lawyers, for which you need to earn certain qualifications before you can fully work in the field. However, in some other fields where a particular degree or certification is not that essential, you do not necessarily need to add more letters behind your name if you are practical and self-confident enough to do the work without the approval a certification gives. However, some people who need certain reinforcement to confidently perform their work can gain a lot of confidence from earning certifications. In this case, I would also recommend them.

We talked about the need to learn both general and technical skills. In my view, it is beneficial for every person no matter their line of work to have a certain breadth of knowledge and a certain depth of expertise. Some people call it a "T-shaped" set of skills. With that, you are able to fit into more than one position and you will be more likely to have innovative ideas when there is a need for it. It makes you more confident to interact with other professionals and helps you to better understand specialists from other areas. Hence, I recommend pursuing both breadth and depth of knowledge.

However, whenever I have to recommend a topic of learning for my direct reports or mentees, I always keep in mind that everyone has their own background of education, learning, and experiences. I only can give them my recommendation and encourage them to seek out other recommendations, but in the end, there is no one better to decide what to pursue than they themselves.

Where to find the time, if not stealing it

In our busy lives, we are not often given free time either at work or in private. Hence, making time to learn is a matter of prioritization. Some people swear by allocating an hour a day for reading and learning, even if they are super busy. Some of the most successful people even attribute their success to this, for example, the entrepreneur and investor Warren Buffett, who said, "The most important investment you can make is in yourself." He also stated, "I insist on a lot of time being spent, almost every day, to just sit and think. That is very uncommon in American business. I read and think. So I do more reading and thinking, and make less impulse decisions than most people in business." Or take it from the highly successful businessman and bestselling author Stephen Covey: "The key to success is dedication to lifelong learning."

My take is that you need to reflect on how much you already learn by experience and interaction on the job. If that is sufficient, you do not need to set aside an extra hour for reading or trainings each and every day. However, what you need to make sure of is that you can relate what you learn to what you do. Having knowledge without practically applying it will not help it stick in your brain, and it might be a lost effort otherwise.

A word of advice to the busiest people in the world, to ambitious, dedicated, full-time working mothers and fathers: There is so much you typically have to squeeze into your day that you rightly will say that you will neither have the time nor the energy to take even five minutes for self-development. In that case, I have something for you. I actually recommend this to less busy people too, and to everyone in fact. After each interaction, be it a meeting, a business discussion with colleagues, or a text you just read, simply ask yourself, *What was the most important insight in that exchange and what have I learned from it?* These short reflections will multiply the effect of learning at work. And please keep in mind, just juggling the many things you have in your life, organizing your schedule and being present wherever you are, brings you so much learning outside of your work that you will find growth and fulfillment.

Learning how to learn

Aside from not allocating the time, another thing that keeps people away from learning is not knowing how to effectively learn. For example, just reading an article or an entire book without deeper reflection is not worth the time spent. If you do not know how to effectively learn, you will learn less, and you may not be motivated to continue the effort of learning at all.

To be an effective learner, you need some understanding of how you learn best. There are ample courses these days where you can learn this. Hence, I only give you my brief view on it here.

It takes time to connect what you have learned to what you already know, whether it is in direct reference to yourself or your environment and daily life. And any new skill must be practiced so that you use it to the fullest potential. People often seem to forget that without repetition and practice, what they learn will most likely not stick in their memory. Even after you gain this insight, learning is still not over. You get the best effect if you exchange what you have learned with others. Whether you talk about it with others, or even teach it to others, or you ask for feedback on a new skill from others, the more you exchange with others around new learning, the better you will understand it yourself and ultimately remember it.

To conclude this section, I would like to say that self-development will take you further in your profession by learning new skills, be they general or specific technical skills. Self-development can include things like developing your values, the quality of your thinking, or anything related to achieving your goals. Doing so will help you increase your awareness and maturity and ultimately lead you to reach your full potential.

Summary

- Lifelong learning is a must and a joy at the same time. In the past few years, progress has accelerated in almost every industry and continues to do so. Therefore, re-skilling and up-skilling have become important for employees to stay relevant. Also, lifelong learning and self-development bring growth and progress, which makes people feel fulfilled and happy.

- There are several types of learners: the ones that learn "on the job," the ones that base their learning on daily news and the media, the very targeted learners, and those who are unable to learn because they think they already know all they need to know.

- There are several types of learning: learning by doing, experiencing by observing and exchanging with others, and formal training, including attending courses, reading books, listening to podcasts, etc.

- Finding time for learning in our busy lives requires prioritization. The easiest way is to be always in learning mode. For instance, after each meeting, a discussion with colleagues, or reading a text, we should ask ourselves: What was the most important insight in that exchange and what have we learned from it?

- Learning how to learn is an important prerequisite for effective learning. It entails reflecting and relating the newly learned knowledge or skill to ourselves and our environment, as well as practicing new skills. We get the best effect if we exchange what we have learned with others, or by getting feedback from others on our new skill.

Exercises

1. What have you learned in your professional life so far? In what areas of your life have you grown? What have you learned in your current position? How have you matured as a person?

2. What would you still want to learn in your current job? Note it down in your personal development plan. In case you already have a formalized plan, make sure it includes these important items. In

any case, make sure you have noted down what experiences, insights from others, and formal learning opportunities you need to seek out in order to achieve your goals.

3. Reflect on the type of learner you are. Are you an exclusively "on the job" learner, or are you a rather coincidental or a more deliberate learner? If you are either an "on the job" learner or a coincidental learner, reflect on how you could become a more targeted learner.

4. Every evening for one work week, write down what you learned that day. At the end of the week, reflect on it all. Have you learned enough? Did you learn something that you would not have noticed if you had not done this exercise? Decide whether you want to go on with this type of conscious, instant learning.

Being present and self-confident

Realize deeply that the present moment is all you will ever have.

—Eckhart Tolle

This is maybe the most important section of the entire book. With all our lofty goals, ambitious plans, earnest work, and busy activities throughout each day, we need to make sure that we enjoy the journey we are on and that we find happiness along the way. We should not postpone happiness for an unknown day in the future when we will have achieved our goals. Say you had a big goal and you have reached it. Then it is easy to be proud and feel a sense of accomplishment. Of course it will make you happy to have reached that goal. However, it cannot be that you only feel a short sensation of happiness after all the hard work, which probably spanned months or even years. It is more the daily achievements along our way that we should celebrate and be thankful for. This means being aware of the journey we are taking and enjoying it at each step, which leads us right into the present moment. Whenever we are fully present in body, mind, and soul, meaning our thoughts are in the same place as we are physically, that we are focused on what we are doing, and that we want to be doing what we are doing, then we enjoy the present moment and our being and doing gets full power. In that moment, we are in flow, which as we learned earlier is incredibly satisfying and makes us feel fulfilled and happy. In fact, happiness can only be experienced in the present moment.

Just as a side note, let us consider for a moment: Why even have goals when we should only be aware of the present moment? We need goals to bring us into directed movement. Remember, life is about expanding happiness, and progress is a large part of this. Wisely chosen goals give us a direction and bring us into flow. In the state of flow, we do not think about the past or the future; we are fully present. When we are too focused on the end goal, that obsession keeps us from enjoying the process to go there and we end up missing the most important parts of life.

And so it is most important to be present. Not being fully present means our thoughts are somewhere else, maybe contemplating a remark a colleague made a few hours ago, or wondering what others may say about the presentation we are working on, or simply thinking of something other than the task before us in that moment. If we are not present in the moment, we lose traction and energy.

Focusing on the past or the future draws us away from the present moment. If we are honest, we do not need to think too often about the past. It is helpful to learn from the past, but once you have done that, it is sufficient. You do not need to relive the same situation over and over to avoid repeating mistakes. Anyway, the past is unchangeable. Too many people let their past steal their present by constantly turning to the same old thoughts. Hence, spend as little time as possible in the past with your mind. Obviously, it makes sense to think about the future from time to time in order to be prepared and make good plans, but consider that it is often the right action in the present that prevents you from making mistakes in the future.

There are people who realize that they have not lived in the present moment for most of their adult lives. While on vacation, they were thinking of home; on their daily walk, they were thinking about the future; when spending time with their children, they were actually pondering business problems. Do not get me wrong—we need to think into the future, and from time to time it is even nice to think about the past. However, only being present makes you feel fully alive. Hence, you should strive to stay in the here and now as much as you can.

Having it all

There is a big debate, particularly among working mothers, about whether one can "have it all." The full package includes being a good parent, having a challenging job, having a fulfilling partnership, and having enough time for yourself, hobbies, and friends. My view is (and you might have already guessed it): Yes, you can have it all, but not all at the same time. I even think that you do not want it all at the same time. Obviously, you are forced to prioritize, but most importantly, what you can or cannot have depends on how you think about it. If you think you cannot have it all, well, it will certainly be true, and you will spend quite some time complaining to yourself and others that you do not have time for all the things you want. If you think the opposite, you need to become aware of a few things. The most important of those is the importance of being present, followed by good organization of your energy and time. Everyone has the same 24 hours to use, and we saw before how important it is to have good energy and time management. The rest, again, is a matter of perspective.

Being present means that you are *really present* where you are. That is, your thoughts are at the place where you physically are, not at another place, or in the past, or in the future. When you are present at work, you are focused on working and not worrying about what terrible thing might happen to your child or spouse somewhere else. When you are at home, you are not worrying and thinking about tasks at work or where else you would rather be. In addition, it helps greatly not to have negative or nagging thoughts about yourself and your working style, or about others and their behavior. With this mindset, you will discover that you have so much more time than you ever thought possible.

As an example, if you have children and you want to be untroubled at work, of course you need well-organized care for your children. Depending on your situation, daycare, a private nanny, or a helpful relative can be the best solution. Most important is that you feel good and safe leaving your children in their care. Only then will you be able to go about your workday worry free. The same goes for when you are together with your children. You should not allow yourself to think about your work and worry whether everything is running as you wanted it to run. If you give your children your full attention and your full love in the time you spend together, it feels good and is much more satisfying than if you are elsewhere in your thoughts. And in exactly these moments, you are the perfect parent you want to be. And when you are back at work, if you are present and if your focus is at work and nowhere else, you are the perfect employee there. The same goes with the time you are spending with your friends or when you are on vacation. Breaks feel much longer when you are fully present, plus you will feel more relaxed and satisfied afterwards.

There is no use in trying to split your attention by dividing your thoughts between different places. Doing so takes a lot of your energy and you will not be able to enjoy any activity to the fullest, because you are not truly present.

To be present during your day, you need to organize it. First, you need to choose how much time you want to spend on each activity. The more conscious you are in deciding this, the better you can accept the fact that, in the end, your time is precious and finite. Then, you do not have to complain that you do not have enough time for your work, your family, your friends, and so on, as the division of it was your deliberate choice. Luckily, less complaining also gives you back the time and energy you would have needed to complain. Fun aside, today is all you have. If you are not present in the moment, you literally can miss your life.

BEING PRESENT

In the early years of my corporate career, I struggled quite a bit with being present. I always tried to squeeze everything into my busy life, mingling thoughts about my private life with those about my business life, as well as thoughts about other people, worries about the future, and so on. When

I first read about the benefits of being present, I did a self-test. I happened to be on a ski vacation where I committed to being fully present at least five times a day. I forced myself to stay in the present moment by keeping my thoughts right where I was, not in the past or the future, nor letting them wander to another place with absent people. Then I held this state for some minutes, up to half an hour. I can tell you, I have never had such a long ski vacation before, although it lasted exactly one week, just like all the trips before it. Although it was many, many years ago, I still remember now the blue sky and the tiny crystals shining on the snow's surface.

By being fully present, you can activate an incredible power for memory. Also, being present leaves no space for negativity. Not being present uses up a lot of your energy and it is obvious that you cannot fully enjoy whatever activities you are doing if you are not truly present in them. Just imagine being fully present all the time, how much time, space, and peace would arise within you.

From my experience, being fully present can also help one make better decisions. For instance, if you have meetings where you need to decide something, remind yourself to be present with your thoughts. You will find it is rather easy. First, it requires the intention to be present. Then, just take a deep breath, concentrating on your body in the region of your heart. Keep breathing slowly and deeply. If this does not bring you into the "here and now" directly, think of yourself being rooted to the spot where you are sitting or standing, like a tree in the woods. After about ten seconds, concentrate on the decision you are about to make. Once you have brought your mind back to an awareness of your body, it will not wander but stay present on the particular subject at hand.

You might have sensed, being present is also a great power and an incredible gift. It is the reason why you do not necessarily need to work long hours or make great personal sacrifice to have a "good" career. Those who are fully present in their work get so much more done that they do not need to put in all the extra time.

Executive presence

Management literature describes a special type of presence called *executive presence*. It means that with your presence, you influence others so that they listen to you, trust you, and potentially follow your advice. But executive presence is not only about talking to others and convincing them to follow your suggestions, but also about attentively listening to others and being genuinely interested to understand their views. It is also about building the space for everyone to actively participate, share opinions freely, and become present as well. People with high executive presence make others feel important so that they are comfortable speaking up. Typically, they are rather calm, do not overreact if something is bothering them, and give the overall impression that they have things under control.

Executive presence is referred to as such because it is the behavior that one would expect from someone in an executive position. However, you do not need to be an executive to show executive presence. Anyone who communicates with others can show this characteristic. People radiating executive presence are typically seen as competent, reliable, and having the potential for great achievements. Other people like to follow them and adopt their suggestions. Hence, they are offered more opportunities, more speaking time in meetings, and more trust in general.

It is important to know that executive presence is not an inherent trait but a skill that can be learned and mastered. The further you are in your career and the more senior you are in your company, the more important executive presence will become for you.

In her insightful book *The Power of Presence: Unlock Your Potential to Influence and Engage Others* (2011), the American communications expert and leadership coach Kristi Hedges explains what is required for executive presence and how you can train it. In particular, she explains that nearly everyone has an excellent presence at times, just maybe not in the professional environment, and that it is often only a matter of transferring that presence to business life. Think of a friend telling you something about his hobby or vacation, or a mother talking about her child; they probably speak with wonderful presence. Transferring this kind of presence to your business life is possible with the right mental attitude, if you have banished limiting thoughts and behaviors, and can communicate in a visionary, inspiring way. Hedges even claims that nothing makes people advance faster in their career than a compelling presence—neither stellar technical knowledge, nor a strong work ethic, nor excellent presentation skills. Hence, you should start cultivating an executive presence early in your career, and work to keep refining it over time.

Some aspects of executive presence Kristi Hedges describes, and which are also deeply rooted principles in this book, are knowing your values and which of them you want to convey, allowing yourself to be authentic, and being intentional about communication. One piece of advice I particularly like is simply to smile more. It improves your presence to others and reinforces good thoughts for yourself.

Executive presence requires assertiveness. For instance, you have to take your space and time in a meeting. Of course, if you are early in your career or new in your job, this might not be the easiest. However, if you believe you belong to the group of people you are with, and if you know what you bring to the table, you can make an impact by simply being present, listening attentively, and posing thoughtful questions. However, if you are dominating the conversation or ignoring what others say, this can diminish your executive presence. Also, it goes without saying that checking mobile devices while in a meeting is destroying your executive presence.

By the way, presence can be contagious. If someone is very present in a meeting, it will draw others to become present too. If you are able to do this, then you have mastered an important aspect of corporate life.

Self-confidence and assertiveness

Self-confidence and assertiveness are important elements of executive presence. We have all experienced that there is nothing more refreshing and easygoing than someone who is self-confident. Of course, self-confidence without competence does not lead people anywhere and it becomes rather tedious to listen to these sorts of people. However, if you are confident and clear in your thinking, others will easily listen to your opinions and what you have to say. You will more easily reach your goals and get ahead at work. Also, research shows that self-confident people are able to establish and maintain happier relationships, build more satisfying careers, and earn more money (Shell 2012). I do not know anyone who would not like to be self-confident.

Unfortunately, not everybody is self-confident in the corporate world. Psychologists have even described the common nagging feeling of not being enough as one of the biggest diseases affecting humanity. The important question is: What can we do to become more self-confident if it is something we struggle with? To answer this, we must first know the reasons for low self-confidence. Low self-confidence can simply come from not being well-prepared or being too much of a perfectionist. However, it can sometimes be more complicated than that, and psychology suggests low self-confidence can come from our cultural background, childhood experiences, family dynamics, societal expectations, relationships, stress, or other life circumstances, all of which are specific to the individual.

There is a special form of low self-confidence sometimes found in very well-educated, fully prepared people who think they are frauds and do not belong where they are. It is called *impostor syndrome* or impostorism, and it is where people persist in believing that they are not good enough despite academic accomplishments and an incredible track record at their workplace. They fear that their colleagues will find out that they are not as capable as they probably thought, or that they have not deserved praise and recognition for something they have accomplished. More than anything, they fear failure. Apparently, impostorism is not that rare and is equally distributed among men and women. It is very uncommon that people talk about it, and so people suffering from impostorism feel alone in their experience. It can be very stressful, as it makes them unconvincing, and they are certainly not living their full potential.

In her insightful book *Presence: Bringing Your Boldest Self to Your Biggest Challenges* (2015), American professor and social psychologist Amy Cuddy provides a thorough background on impostorism, as well as tips for how to overcome low self-confidence. Among other things, she claims that our body language influences others and can even change the way we see ourselves. In particular, she suggests doing power poses before important talks, interviews, or meetings, or even once a day in order to train the mind to believe what we are really capable of. A power pose means standing in a posture of confidence like hands at the hips, expanding chest and shoulders. Cuddy claims acting powerfully makes you begin to think powerfully. With that, our confidence level rises. Unfortunately, some of her research was not reproducible, such as her findings about power posing having the ability to change the chemicals in the brain, but it was at least possible to reproduce the pattern that power posing helps people overcome fear of failure.

Other self-confidence boosting measures include concentrating on positive thoughts rather than negative ones, reminding ourselves of and standing by our values, and being together with positive people.

The good news is that acting confidently does not necessarily require you to feel fully confident. To become self-confident, first and foremost you need to become present. If you are presenting something and at the same time you are thinking about what impression you are making on your listeners and what possible outcomes might be, your presence and skills are diminished. You will not have enough focus and your memory will not work at the optimal level. You can stop this constant self-monitoring by becoming present. As we heard earlier, thinking positively, rather than negatively, also helps. Positive affirmations on how intelligent and competent you are support self-confidence as well. Generally, surrounding yourself with positive people makes you think more positively too.

In my view, self-confidence is your birthright. Over time, however, many of us have buried our confidence under limiting beliefs. Praise raises self-confidence greatly. If, for whatever reason, you do not get enough praise from others, quietly praise yourself often. With self-confidence you respect yourself, you believe in your abilities and strengths, and you feel positive about yourself. Then, others will more likely have confidence in you too. Hence, you will be able to more easily handle challenges and reach your goals. It is a positive spiral.

When you are self-confident, it is much easier to be assertive too. Assertiveness brings a lot of clarity to your interactions with others because you express your opinions openly. It gives you control over what you want, and you can stand up for yourself as needed.

As with self-confidence, assertiveness is a skill that can be learned. It has some prerequisites, though, such as knowing the facts about the matter at hand and being aware of your own abilities. Then, you have to be prepared to answer potential questions and be prepared with questions for others. All this requires remaining calm and respectful in case someone challenges you. If that occurs, just tell the other person how you feel and what you want to see done differently. Assertive people respect others, and also themselves. Having control over a situation is life mastery too.

If you want to advance your career and take on a more senior position, you need executive presence. If you assess yourself to be lacking it, or see that you are not where you would like to be, you either need to build up your knowledge and experience or your self-confidence, or both. If you are early in your career, try to acquire knowledge first, as experience only comes with time. However, if what you lack is self-confidence, try to address it as soon as you can. As we learned earlier in the book, what we express on the outside is often a reflection of what we have inside of us. Sheryl Sandberg, an American business executive, said, "Nobody gets a promotion who does not think they deserve their success." This is exactly the point. You have to work on your own feelings of worthiness to get what you want.

Summary

- The present moment is all we really have.

- Being present in the moment means being present with body, mind, and soul, meaning we are in our thoughts at the same place where we physically are. We are concentrating on what we are doing.

- Not being present uses a lot of our energy and we will not be able to enjoy our activities to the fullest.

- In the business environment, executive presence is very powerful. It is the ability to influence others so that they listen to you, trust you, and potentially follow your advice. It is about attentively talking and listening, and about building the space so that everyone actively participates, shares opinions freely, and becomes present as well.

- Executive presence is not a trait but a skill that can be learned and mastered. The further you are in your career or the more senior you are at your company, the more important executive presence will become.

- High self-confidence is a part of executive presence and makes it easier for you to reach your goals and get ahead at work.

- Praise raises our self-confidence greatly. Hence, praise yourself often.

Exercises

1. In order to practice presence, write on a card the word "NOW" and place it somewhere visible on your desk. Have a look once in a while throughout your workday and take a moment to simply be. This does not need to be for long. In this moment of presence, consciously choose a thought that gives you strength now, and enjoy the effect of that thought. This ultra-simple action has a big impact on your consciousness. Among other benefits, it will make you feel that you have more time.

2. Being in the present moment is not always easy. Some people literally have to learn to do it. If you have difficulty being truly present, meditation can help. So can the following small exercise: Do the following at least once a day. It only takes three minutes in total.

a. Take one minute to look at something you have in front of you. It can be an item like a pencil, your coffee mug, your purse, or whatever is around. It can also be your finger or a tree or a cloud you see in the sky. Look at it as if you are seeing it for the first time. See every little scratch or groove, the texture, the color, and so on. Do it so intensely that you do not have time to think about anything else. Stop after one minute.

b. Then, close your eyes and take one minute to hear whatever sounds happen to be around you. Start with the sounds outside of your building. Maybe you can hear church bells, sirens, airplanes, or other traffic. Then listen to the sounds within your building. Maybe you can hear the steps or voices of other people. Then listen to what you hear in your room. Maybe there are people close by, or the white noise of a ceiling fan, or the buzz of a light. Gradually come closer to yourself. In the end, you should hear your breath and potentially the sound of your blood in the ears. Stop again after one minute.

c. Still keeping your eyes closed, take one minute to feel within your body. How your feet are touching the ground, which parts of your body are touching your chair, or bed, or wherever you are. Feel the whole body and notice where you feel tension or where you feel good. Maybe you feel even the tingling in your fingertips.

In the beginning, you can set a timer to measure out one minute per task. Soon, you will get a good feel for how long a minute of observing is. This short, three-minute exercise will bring you fully into the present moment.

Do not be surprised if you come to new realizations through this exercise. When you focus your mind, or rather force it into the present, it relaxes completely, and good ideas just fly to you afterwards.

After a week of doing this exercise once a day, reflect on how it has changed your perception of the present. If you feel you do not have time for meditation, this exercise is a great alternative to sense the present moment. If you found benefit in it, seriously consider adding it to your daily schedule in the future. Or you can come back to this exercise during stressful times.

3. This is an exercise to improve self-confidence: Remember a specific time you felt totally confident. It can be at work or in your personal life. Think back on what it was and even more about the way it felt. What did you do exactly? Try to remember every detail. How did it feel deep inside? Now, take a recent situation where you would have wished to be more self-confident. Drawing inspiration from your

earlier memory, how could you have appeared more confident? How would it have felt? Think of someone whom you perceive as supremely confident. What would this person have done differently?

The next time you find yourself in a similar situation of wanting to boost your confidence, for instance before a meeting or a big presentation, prepare yourself by remembering the feeling of confidence.

Being aware of self-confidence, you can also formulate an affirmation to carry around for a while, such as "I am truly confident," "Confidence is my birthright," or simply "I am enough."

4. If you would like to boost your executive presence, try to first become clear on how you are perceived by others. Seek out feedback from someone whose opinion you trust. Ask them their first impressions of you. Ask them to describe you in five words. Where do they see your strengths and weaknesses? Their responses may lead you to areas you can further improve. Then, make a development plan for yourself that accounts for your strengths and weaknesses. Work particularly on your strengths, as doing so will make you more of who you are. You will radiate more authenticity and presence, which will make you more successful overall.

Chapter 4

ON RELATIONSHIP MANAGEMENT

On networks

The time to build a network is always before you need one.

—Douglas Conant

Humans are social beings who like to be around and exchange ideas with others. They have a fundamental need to belong, to have positive interpersonal exchange and lasting relationships. Hence, we naturally build networks with the people we know and interact with. Everyone has a network. Even the loneliest and most withdrawn people have a network, though it may be small. At the other end of the spectrum, there are people who have a huge network and almost their whole day seems to consist of networking. Most people are in between these extremes—some love networking, some like it less. However, this does not necessarily speak to the size of their network. The effort you put into your networking is not always proportional to the size or efficiency of your network. In fact, conscious networking may bring you a solid network that is not too time consuming to build and maintain. It is simply a matter of focusing your efforts.

But let us first start with some definitions. A *network* consists of a set of individuals who are connected by interpersonal relationships. Through their network, people may get answers to their questions and general information to help them accomplish things. They get input in the form of advice, insights, new ideas, feedback, and potentially support and resources for what they want to achieve. The benefits can range as far as transacting business, developing professionally, and getting ahead in their career. Networks also help people to expand their influence and have more impact.

Types of networks

Typically, people distinguish between personal and professional networks, and the two can overlap. There is a more helpful categorization described by Herminia Ibarra, professor of organizational behavior at London Business School, in her great book *Act Like a Leader, Think Like a Leader* (2015). She divides networks into *personal, operational,* and *strategic* networks. Your *operational network* consists of people at work. This network is primarily there to help you get your work done efficiently. The key contacts are those you work with daily to complete your work tasks and are further determined by organizational structure. It is very clear who is relevant. Your *personal network* consists of friends, family, former classmates, and maybe colleagues or people you know from other professional associations with whom you share a degree of closeness. This network is there to enhance personal and also professional development, and these people can typically refer you to useful information and contacts. It is not always clear who is relevant in one's personal network, but you decide who is in this circle or not. Then, your *strategic network* consists of contacts from work or outside whose acquaintance you keep in order to stay oriented toward the future. This network is there to help you figure out future priorities and challenges and to provide support. Here, it is not always clear who is relevant, but generally, this form of network gives you a link to the outside or your daily world.

Whereas operational and personal networks are easy and almost natural to build, establishing and maintaining a strategic network takes deeper reflection and more effort. It is the form of network that is easily overlooked in our daily lives. The strategic network often consists of people you do not necessarily encounter all the time, and these people are typically of different backgrounds. In contrast, personal and operational networks are more closed networks, where you rather are connected to people because you are in the same industry or personally know each other well.

STRATEGIC NETWORKING

For a while in my own corporate life, I reported to an extremely bright, highly successful, and business-savvy CEO. He was not only professionally but also personally an outstanding person. Upon entering his office, you immediately noticed that he had nothing on his desk but his computer, the keyboard, the telephone, and sometimes one or two sheets of paper he was working on or that required his signature. On the bottom corner of his computer screen, though, he had a small sticky note with a few names on it. These were the people he regularly called. I spotted a handful of names on it, like the chairman of our company's supervisory board, the CEO and CFO of the holding company, as well as a few CEOs of friendly competitors and one or two industry makers. These were mostly people from his strategic network, and that sticky paper acted as a visual reminder to help him maintain his strategic network.

Now, a question: When is a person really in your network and when are they not? Personally, I consider people in my closer network if I reliably get an answer from them, and likewise if I reliably respond to their requests. Most of us have hundreds to thousands of contacts on LinkedIn or other social media. However, if I make a suggestion to get lunch with someone and this person says, "Yes, let's aim for some time next month," and if I ask a month later and the person does not answer, then this person is clearly not in my closer network, although we are connected through a social network. It is the same with unanswered messages. Obviously, these people do not feel I belong to their closer network or else they would answer.

This makes me sometimes wonder why they wanted to be connected at all. Anthropological research has an explanation for this behavior. Studies show that human beings cannot build stable social relationships with more than 100 to 150 people (some say up to 250) maximum (Dunbar 2016). This explains why some people out of our social media networks of 500+ connections do not respond to our queries. We are outside of the number of people they can cope with. However, this does not exclude that you occasionally get answers from those people, but you will not get them reliably. But do not underestimate what people at the periphery of your network, those who are not too close to you, can do for you still. They can be instrumental in helping you find a new job or connecting you with other people.

Interesting research around networks

Some years ago, when I was preparing my mentoring circles, I came across highly interesting research around networks, which, when I first heard it, stunned me. I became convinced then that everyone should know about it. In the meantime, there has been further research done on the topic that I also would like to present to you here, as I consider it to be crucial knowledge.

There is research going back decades that says the people we like to be with, we easily bring into our network. We network with people who are similar to us. Some people refer to it as the "likes attract" principle, or *affinity bias*; however, the technical term is "homophily," which combines the Ancient Greek words for "together" and "friendship" or "love." A vast number of studies have shown that similarity is associated with connection. Human beings naturally like to be together with others that have something in common with them, be it similarity in social class, organizational role, education, religion, or values, but the similarities can also be very basic, such as race, age, or gender.

My guess is that you have experienced this and can recall instances where you searched for similarities with people you met for the first time and felt good when you found a point of connection. If nothing comes to mind, look at your close friends—chances are, you share some important things in common.

Let us dive deep into *homophily and gender*. When I deeply realized what homophily in this context means, I changed my mind with regards to professional quotas. Whereas in the past, I found quotas somewhat artificial and not very flattering for women who probably were hired to fill a quota, I later realized that quotas are needed and even indispensable if you want to change gender equity in committees or higher-level management in a corporation.

WHEN NETWORKING IS DIFFICULT

I once gave a presentation to some young women about the career benefits of networking. After the presentation, one of the women came up to me and asked for personal advice. She worked in a very technical field with mostly male colleagues and almost no women in higher positions. She said that she tried networking with more senior people and also colleagues of the same level by asking them to lunch. However, her male colleagues were reluctant to have a meal with her because, on one hand, it annoyed them because they did not know what to talk about with her, and on the other hand, they were afraid she had hidden motives about starting a romantic relationship. This young lady was desperate because she was very ambitious and eager to climb the company hierarchy, and also because she simply wanted to be seen and accepted by her colleagues. I realized that her chances for networking were significantly worse than her male colleagues, and the only thing I could offer her directly was to link her to other senior women outside her department. In addition, I recommended that she volunteer to work on projects throughout her department so that more people got to know her.

If you think it through, it is absolutely no wonder that you will not get gender balance in higher ranks if you do not force it. People like to promote people they know. Due to affinity bias, people like to network with people similar to them. Just think about who goes to lunch with whom, or who lingers to chat five minutes longer with whom after a meeting. Typically, it is people who are similar to each other, people who, at first glance, have more topics to talk about and relate on. It is people who easily agree with each other. Hence, homophily, being such a strong force, ultimately is decisive in regard to career success.

In my opinion, it is not enough to just raise awareness about affinity bias to achieve gender balance in higher ranks, although it certainly helps. There needs to be an organized effort to level the playing field of who gets promoted. Of course, this applies not only to gender, but also to race, beliefs and ways of thinking, and other forms of diversity.

Still on the topic of gender, other research by Herminia Ibarra shows that women have a different approach to networking than men. This may ultimately also be attributed to affinity bias and the lack of women in higher ranks, but it has been shown that women have a more stringent separation between their personal and operational networks than men do. For men, there is usually a lot of overlap between the operational network and the personal network. They play sports together with their coworkers or get together for a barbecue with the others working on an important business project. Women typically get together more with family- or neighborhood-related contacts for their private activities, oftentimes also through the network around their children's friends and activities. Also, women tend to first think about what they can give to a network partner and are reluctant to ask for something when they do not see a direct benefit for the other person. However, if you think back to the maximum 150 people you can have in your closer network, men tend to have a dramatically larger operational network.

ENJOY YOUR NETWORK

In my corporate life, I once knew a local CEO of a larger organization who, when he turned fifty, organized a huge party. He invited 200 people to the party that had a full program that spanned a whole weekend. Wondering about the size of his private network, I asked him whom he had invited. He said he invited family, friends, coworkers, clients, and other business partners. I gave this some serious thought. Up until that point in my own life, the thought of inviting clients and business partners to a private birthday party was beyond my realm of imagination. At least, I would never have considered it for myself. However, reflecting on it, I concluded that having his large network would make it likely that this CEO would never have problems finding another job should he be laid off or otherwise need a change. Besides, if you are a person who loves big parties, all the better.

Let us now deep dive into *homophily and age*. These days, diversity in age has become an important issue in the workplace. You can almost divide a workforce into digital natives and non-digital natives, where digital natives are naturally more savvy and better versed in all the newest devices, internet trends, and social media than the generations before. Of course, technological fluency is not the only distinction separating younger and older generations. Due to homophily, each generation, both young and old, tends to stick together. Hence, it is more difficult for the older generation to understand what the younger generation can deliver or what may come next in technological innovation. Likewise, the younger generation has difficulty understanding how business really works with the older generation, who still largely hold important company positions. Those precious people who understand both groups, because they have relevant representants in their networks, are particularly valuable for a company.

Research shows that being in an open network instead of a closed one is a good predictor of career success (Burt 1995). An *open* network consists of people who do not know each other, who possibly are from various industries, whereas a *closed* network consists mainly of people who are all interconnected and know each other. In fact, having an open network is a larger indicator of success than promotion, compensation, or industry recognition. This is understandable, as in a closed network the same ideas are quickly spread and repeated, and no one has a competitive advantage. Hence, the people bringing information from one closed group to another—because they have an open network—are particularly valuable in each network. However, people with open networks might not have the easiest role in each of their respective closed networks, as building trust and understanding is easier within a closed group.

Another interesting piece of research by Herminia Ibarra looks at how our networks help us to change and become who we want to be. Research shows that "the fastest way to change yourself is to spend time with people who are already the way you want to be." Hence, whenever your role expands, for instance when you are entering a new leadership position or taking on a larger assignment, then spending your time with people who are already at that level or are doing what you aspire to do will help you succeed in your new role.

Let me finish by talking about "social capital," another widely researched topic. There is far too much research to reference all of it here. However, *social capital* is defined in the Oxford Dictionary as "the network of relationships among people who live and work in a particular society, enabling that society to function effectively." Practically, this means that if you have a higher social capital than someone else, you have a larger network of people who are likely to help you. Research shows that those people who are perceived to have high social capital are more likely to get help as well as have better access to resources and critical information, for instance for project work. In general, they get more instrumental support, meaning that they get more time, resources, and important advice when they ask for it. It even seems to be the case that women are more likely to help men than they are to help other women because of social capital. As a result, people with higher social capital have a better chance of being promoted and, in the end, earn more.

I am sure you know people with higher social capital than others. Remember, it is not the sheer size of your network that counts but the number of people who are likely to help you. To increase this, you need to build trust with these people by repeatedly interacting with them, following through on commitments, behaving consistently, and communicating honestly.

Networking has a fundamental impact on every single stage of your career development. Hence, there is no way around building a good network, whether you use it for business or personally. But especially if you want to become or if you already are a leader, it is of utmost importance to have a good network. Some people even go as far as saying that for someone striving to become a leader, the alternative to networking is failure, which is to say that without a strong network, you will either not get the leadership position you aspire to, or if you do get it, you will not succeed at it.

Consciously building your network

There are many ways to build your network. Some people like networking events, some like being active through social media, and others prefer mainly taking a natural approach of just letting connections organically build as they come. Some people even claim they do not do any networking at all, as they have absolutely no time for it. However, every personal interaction with others has some aspect of networking, so doing no networking at all is just impossible.

Many people understand networking as something formal, like going to specific networking events, gatherings, or conferences. The way I understand networking does not have much to do with events and the acquaintances I might possibly make there. I simply understand networking as the interaction I have with the individuals in my network as well as the buildup of my network. It has also no connotation of judgement or false pretenses.

Some people find the idea of networking to be manipulative and even insincere, as they feel it would be "using" people, or they fear someone may find they have ulterior motives. People in particular dislike building networks for "instrumental" reasons, meaning for instance for further promotions or next jobs. Also, they feel it is a burden to ask for a favor without being able to give one back immediately.

Please keep in mind, the more you realize the "natural law of giving," which postulates that the more you are giving, the more you are receiving, you will appreciate that being able to give is actually a gift for the giver. Hence, whenever someone does you a favor, it is ultimately a gift for this person too. With that, you will understand that giving and receiving in networks is the same good thing and makes people happy on both ends of the exchange.

Research also shows that the more senior a person is in a firm, the more comfortable they become with networking. They see it as beneficial and exciting rather than inauthentic, uncomfortable, or even dirty (Ibarra

2015). This has to do with the fact that more senior people believe they have something valuable to give.

From my personal experience, I can fully confirm that research finding. I became more comfortable and joyful in networking over time. But please keep in mind, even when you are at the very start of your career, you have valuable things to give. It may be that your insights are of interest to the other party, or you may have information they do not have. Some may even see it as a gift to share their experience, mentor, or teach you.

GROWING A NETWORK

Looking back, I built my strategic network somewhat by chance rather than very consciously. But looking at it now, it amazes me how broad my network actually is, in particular my strategic network. I was lucky because my profession literally forced me to build a diverse strategic network. As a Chief Risk Officer, you need to have knowledge and an opinion about pretty much everything that goes on in the company, the industry, the economy, the environment, the planet, and the future. Hence, I intuitively reached out to individuals across all kinds of industries. But it is not only from a professional point of view that I have built a strategic network. It is also from a personal standpoint that I can find a person of almost any occupation in my network, reach out to them, and get a reliable answer. However, my network came to me rather unconsciously, and building it with more intentionality would probably have taken less time.

If you have limiting beliefs about networking, it is important that you get rid of them as soon as possible. See networking as something joyful and interesting! Only then will your network become relevant and really helpful to you.

Some people claim that networking is a luxury they cannot afford due to time constraints. However, you need to realize that building a network is also an investment for the future, for the time you will most need it, be it for making your next career move, evaluating innovative ideas, or getting new ideas when you find yourself stuck. The more you see the benefits of a solid network, the more you will also see the urgency to start earlier rather than later.

Building up a solid network takes some effort and time. As we have seen, it is not recommended to only have a network of close contacts from your current work environment. It makes sense to have an open and diverse network, with respect to gender, age, and profession. On the one hand, it is easy to understand that it is not recommended to have hundreds of contacts in a closed network, since it takes a lot of time to build and maintain such a network, but since most people in a closed network tend to know each other, it does not bring many new insights either. On the other hand, research shows one can also have too much diversity in a network, meaning that having a too open network where no one knows each other will make it hard to give and get dependable referrals (Ibarra 2015).

Coming back to the observation that women have different types of networks than men, does this mean that men and women should network differently? We saw that women traditionally have less overlap between their operational and personal networks and might have less easy contact with senior businesspeople due to affinity bias. Hence, when it comes to getting instrumental help through their network, women are at a certain disadvantage. In order to overcome this, my view is that women need to network more consciously and not let their network build only organically. I have three suggestions for this:

- First, women should reach out to women in higher positions. When women lack deeper connections to senior employees, they have a hard time getting more senior jobs, because they are not well known enough.

- Second, women should build networks outside their own company, but in the same industry. Doing so opens them up to valuable input for their work and can increase their social capital.

- Third, women should consider finding work colleagues to spend some of their private time with, as this will enlarge their closer operational/

private network—not to mention, it is probably fun too. Remember, we spend too much time at work to not have a good and fulfilling time there as well.

A short word on women's networks within companies: Some larger companies have built formal networks for women to get to know each other and for senior women of the company to give presentations to other women. I do see some interest in joining these networks, but the support women get through these events is less instrumental and more of social value. Hence, women are more likely to meet people who support them socially, but not sponsors who can really help them advance in their careers. Women even have to be cautious not to have negative, complaining conversations there that will make them feel isolated in their workplace.

When it comes to general networking events like conferences, industry events, or breakfasts, feel free to attend if you like them. If you do not like them, then consciously go only once in a while and get the best out of it. Be very present at the event, not occupied with your phone or writing emails during the talks. During the breaks, do not talk to your work colleagues or people you already know well, but concentrate on meeting people you do not know yet. And the more you are actively contributing to such an event, for instance giving a talk or being part of a discussion panel, or by simply asking a good question after a presentation, the better and easier networking will feel afterwards. The more you make yourself known by speaking up, the easier it is for people to connect with you.

Most importantly, do not feel bad about not going to every networking event because, after all, how you network has to fit your style. However, the less you like networking, the more you need to do it with intention, so that you get more done in less time.

Also, do not underestimate what friends, even those with whom you no longer have much contact, can do for you. If you understand your existing network of friends, you can expand it from there, as it seems that the greatest support for new ideas comes from reaching out to old friends, also called "weak ties" (Burkus 2018). They can introduce you to their contacts whom you might want to know, which makes networking so much easier.

A good way to enlarge your operational network is by volunteering on projects and assignments within your company. By doing so, you get exposure to people you would not typically cross paths with and you have the potential to build a deep relationship over working on the project together. These relationships tend to be close, as work is intense and you have to interact with your teammates quite a bit.

One more important note: When you have met someone you wanted to be introduced to or you have asked someone for a favor, it is advisable to send a thank-you note afterwards, especially if you have just met the person for the first time. In any case, you must follow up with whatever you promised the person, for instance sending a piece of information or article. This builds trust, which is needed to build up a reliable network.

Maintaining your network

An important part of networking is maintaining the relationships you have established. You cannot expect that you meet a person once and they will then reliably answer questions later on when you most desperately need it. You need to take opportunities beforehand to maintain your network, whether you need it or not.

Nowadays, it is easier than ever to maintain and expand your network thanks to professional and business-related social media platforms such as LinkedIn, XING, and others. Such platforms allow people to build business networks, find customers, partners, and clients. They make it easy to stay in contact virtually.

However, these tools do not replace maintaining a network in person, as building trust is better done face to face. Remember, building trust is key to getting reliable responses from your network. But it is not always easy to maintain our networks in person because we are all busy and cannot attend every opportunity or event. Particularly parents with young children lack the time to network after work because they are busy with family life. To maintain my network during busy times, I have met many of my contacts over lunch, or an afternoon coffee or tea together, or by sending them notes about common topics of interest. As a manager, walking around the office can also be an alternative.

I learned when talking to my mentees that another hindering factor that made them feel uncomfortable networking was not knowing what to talk about.

BE PREPARED FOR NETWORKING

When I was younger, the truth is that I was not at all comfortable networking with senior executives. However, I had already realized back then that networking was the key to being known by the decision makers. So when I was invited to a business event or had extra time after an important meeting with some stakeholders, I always thought in advance about what I could talk about. I had sort of a cheat sheet in my head with the top five topics, either from my daily work or the latest industry news. This helped me feel more comfortable approaching others. These days are long gone, but I recall feeling afterwards that pushing myself to have such encounters was definitely worth it, because networking also means getting insights from others, and I often got refreshing views that I could use in my work.

Dale Carnegie, the iconic American motivational writer and speaker, said, "You can make more friends in two months by becoming interested in other people than you can in two years by trying to get other people interested in you." Oftentimes, asking a good question about the other person is an easy start of a conversation with someone you do not know. People love to talk about themselves, so if you want to engage, start asking about them, their career, their family, and so on. Also, sharing positive emotional experiences with people who are quite different from yourself is a good way to connect.

You do not have the same level of relationship with everyone in your network. Some relationships are more superficial, while others can be quite profound. You may apply the 80/20 rule here, meaning that 20 percent of your network will give you 80 percent of value when needed. Hence, take comfort in knowing that you can concentrate on a smaller part of your network to build meaningful, deeper relationships. More than likely, those people will matter in your life, and they will help you out when you need it most.

Just keep in mind that connections are good for all human beings. When we connect with one another, we feel less lonely, depressed, and fearful. Being surrounded with people from our close network who support and challenge us makes our life more colorful, positive, and happy.

Research even comes out in favor of having friends at work. This is a much-debated topic, where opponents have the fear that friendships in corporations may have a negative effect on productivity and might fuel gripe and gossip. But a Gallup study showed that people with friends at work are more likely to be engaged and have higher job satisfaction, which leads to better performance overall (Gallup 2017).

The question remains: How often should we reach out to stay meaningful in someone's network? In my view, this depends on both of your person-alities. You may have friends whom you have not seen for years because of work or living very far apart, but when you meet again, you connect very easily. And you may have business connections who hardly remember you when you see them a second time. In my view, a good schedule is to catch up with the closer network at least two to three times a year. Obviously, you then would spend more time doing something with your friends than with people from your operational network, where lunch appointments are quite common and sufficient for maintaining those connections. However, there are people you might not contact very often and still, they might reliably help you because you have built up a trustful relationship in the past. For those who have only limited time to network, sending a message pointing out an interesting article or podcast or sharing interesting news is another way to catch up. You need to figure out what sort of catching up is necessary with whom in your network.

A good way to stay in contact with people is through social media, for example when you post on LinkedIn or similar business networks with topics you are interested in or when you comment on other people's posts. Again, this is not everyone's favorite, but you need to find out for yourself what is the most effective way to do your networking.

To encourage you to start networking seriously, I want to cite Herminia Ibarra's advice for leaders: "Networking is a lot like nutrition and fitness: we know what to do, the hard part is making it a top priority. And the only way to become convinced that networking is a priority is to start doing it and see the results for yourself."

Just remember that it is your own responsibility to build your network. No one else can do it for you. Find out what works best for you. The less naturally networking comes for you and the more reservations you have about it, the more consciously you need to approach it. And keep in mind that joy comes with doing it in your own way. Personally, I enjoy networking the most when I can help other people through my network, be it by referring people to someone who can give them input for their business, connecting people with similar interests who do not know each other yet, or helping someone find a new job.

Summary

- Networking is important for sharing knowledge, getting support or resources, and facilitating innovation.

- Networks can be divided into three types: personal, operational, and strategic. Whereas the operational network consists of people at work, the personal network consists of family, friends, former colleagues, and others. The strategic network can consist of people at work or outside, but includes people who may be relevant for getting support or insights for figuring out future priorities and challenges.

- "Homophily" or "affinity bias" means that people tend to gravitate toward and network with others who are similar to them. However, this leads to homogeneous networks which typically do not bring enough new ideas and insights.

- Research shows that being in an open network instead of a closed one, where people know each other, is a good predictor of career success.

- Our networks help us change and become who we want to be by spending our time with people who are already at that level or are doing what we aspire to do.

- "Social capital" describes the value of someone's network. The higher your social capital, the more likely you are to get instrumental support in the form of others' time, resources, and important advice. People with higher social capital have a better chance of being promoted and earning more.

- Building and maintaining a network takes time. However, you can save time if you network consciously, for example, by overlapping private and company networks, being fully present at a few networking events, or voluntarily participating in internal company projects and assignments.

Exercises

1. Do you have negative beliefs about networking? If yes, take two sheets of paper. On the first one, you write down your limiting, negative beliefs. On the second, write your supporting, positive beliefs. Think about where the negative beliefs come from. In case they are linked with low self-confidence, consider the exercises about raising self-confidence in the previous chapters.

   In case your negative beliefs prevail, find new, positive ones. Write them on the second sheet of paper and throw away the first sheet in any case. Look at the new positive beliefs from time to time. If you would like to make an effort to network, look at it daily over the time of a few weeks and formulate goals and next steps.

2. Write down at least twenty-five or more people from your network and note which network category they fall into (personal, operational, strategic). Some may fall into two or even all three categories.

Reflect on the quality of your network:

- Who is similar to you?

- Who among your contacts knows each other?

- Is the list all old contacts from earlier phases of your life or are there also new contacts that may lead you into the future?

- In your strategic network, are there many contacts from within your company or also outside ones?

Note how often you have seen each person in the past. Also note down how often you ideally would like to see them or talk to them going forward.

With regards to your strategic network, make a top ten list and place it somewhere you see it from time to time. This should remind you to seek out opportunities to catch up with them.

Do the same with the people from your operational network. Check the list regularly, for instance once a month or every two months, to see whether you met the people you actually wanted to see.

Reflect also on whom else you have seen or met recently and whether you want to add them to your networks. Also think about where you would like to enlarge your network. Make sure you network with people senior and junior to you, and both inside and outside your company.

3. Is there a person you would like to be introduced to? Find someone who knows this person and ask them to make the connection. Before you meet the person, prepare a few interesting conversation topics. Maybe you have a specific question you would like to ask. Maybe check LinkedIn or any other business social media beforehand to learn their interests. Also think about what information you could give to *them.* Perhaps you have insights they do not yet have or you could introduce them to someone interesting from your network.

More simply, give them a compliment. Also, try to find similarities in advance and plan to talk about them.

4. Think about whether you know any people who do not know each other yet but would be a good match because they share similar interests and challenges. Make the introduction and encourage them to exchange ideas. It will help you a lot to understand the power of networking.

On personal career development

The road to happiness lies in two simple principles; find what it is that interests you and that you can do well, and when you find it put your whole soul into it, every bit of energy and ambition and natural ability you have.

—John D. Rockefeller

You may wonder why I talk about career development as part of the relationship management chapter and not the self-management chapter. While you are, of course, at the center of your own career and it is always you who must decide on your next steps, you depend on many other people to achieve your career aspirations.

Depending on where in the world you live, "making a career" has slightly different connotations. It ranges from progressing through life and doing a series of jobs during your work life, to advancing in your work life to earn more money and take on more responsibility. I think of it as the series of jobs you do throughout your life. Consequently, literally everyone who works makes a career.

The question is, then, *what is a good career?* In my view, a particularly good career is one that is driven by growth—that is, growth in knowledge and responsibility as well as personal growth. Additionally, a good career will become a successful career when it leads you into abundance. And we all know that abundance is not only wealth and money. There is much more to it, like your own health, good relationships and, let us not forget, good self-confidence. That is why someone who has worked himself half to death and sacrificed his health to move up a few levels in the hierarchy has not yet had a successful career. Also, someone who has advanced far but cannot be him- or herself, that is, he or she has to pretend every day in order to succeed, has not yet managed to have a successful career. I am sure that even people who have made a lot of money but sacrificed relationships along the way will agree that they have not had a truly satisfying career.

Career planning

Depending on who you ask, you will get different answers about whether a career can be planned or not. Every person requires a different amount of planning in order to feel safe, unless they have a crystal-clear intuition which guides them from one moment to the next. Hence, it is recommended to specify some goals you want to achieve. Along your way, career opportunities will come up that will move you closer to your goals, and new goals will also arise along the way.

Some people swear by getting as many different experiences as possible by changing jobs every two to three years in their early career, while others find it more important to directly try to climb the corporate ladder within one company, area, or field of expertise. In my view, this all does not really matter if you are clear about what you would like to achieve. We talked earlier about your personal North Star, which is aligned with your values and who you are.

I believe that even people who do not know their North Star, and therefore do not consciously follow it, will walk their way towards it. They may meander instead of going straight, and it may well be that they do not realize their full potential in their work lifetime. Nevertheless, their path will lead them somewhere after a few years where they can use their talents, independent of the industry and profession they have chosen. Let me give an example of what I mean. If someone's talent is structuring and organizing, then they are going to end up somewhere structuring and organizing things, whether it is in a financial services company or a pharmaceutical company, whether it is in the accounting department or the research department of a corporation, or in a school or a hospital. They will structure and organize things wherever they land.

From this we learn two things: If you want to fulfill your true potential, you must find your North Star as early as possible and make purposeful steps towards it. But more importantly, if you cannot locate your North Star right this moment, do not spend forever trying to find it, but continue to make steps forward in the meantime. Moving forward in an uncertain direction will still bring you further than standing still waiting for the day when you have finally found out where you want to go. While moving forward, you will learn things about where you want to go, whereas you will not achieve much while waiting. Achieving things along the way will make you feel good, and the more you like what you are doing, the more you will feel fulfilled.

When we are not sure in what direction to go, we often choose the path of least resistance, such as following the company flowchart to the next promotion or the next role up the ladder. There is nothing wrong with following a career path specified by your company, as long as it is in line with your goals. Looking into the future, though, because of economic and technological advancements, it is doubtful whether you can plan a career over decades. Independent of whether you follow your company's career program or not, you are the one who is in charge of managing your career. We talked about this earlier: You are 100 percent responsible for your life. You are responsible for the way you want to work, your career satisfaction, your work-life balance, your personal achievements. Do not wait for someone to approve or give you permission to go forward, otherwise you risk living a shadow version of yourself.

How to choose or change your career

We live in a world of unprecedented opportunities. This makes it difficult to choose what we want to do in our lives. We all need to choose what we will be doing. The more consciously we make this choice, the better. Remember that expanding happiness comes from being fulfilled, which itself comes from doing work we love and find meaningful. The prerequisite for finding what you love is having an understanding about who you are, what strengths and weaknesses you have, and what your most important values are. Doing what you can do well, what you love and enjoy, and applying it to something that contributes to society and helps others is the optimal basis for your career. Using your talent to make others' lives better, safer, and more enjoyable gives meaning to your life. Then your work will generate value. It will not feel like hard work, because the sense of purpose you feel fuels your energy, because you want to do this work, and because it feels very natural to do this work. With that, chances are high that you will become very good at what you have chosen to do and hence your work will generate even more value.

Having competence in something is important. I would not recommend aspiring to be only a generalist. Finding a specialty that differentiates you from others is very valuable. But whatever it is, it needs to give you joy.

We all know people who are enthusiastic about their work. They love what they do, and over time, they became really good at it. They radiate competence and people seek out their services and advice. You should try to find something that genuinely interests you so much that you find it enjoyable to learn and gain experience in it. It will make your days exciting. Your self-confidence will rise, and success tends to follow naturally.

As we live our life and gain more experience, things will change, as by putting in time and effort we become more skilled in what we do. We will reach goals, our horizon will expand, and we will get a deeper understanding of the world. On our way to fulfilling our potential, we will realize that even our potential will expand. Everything in this world is expanding.

It is high time to think about ways to move forward if you feel stuck and seemingly nothing moves forward; you do not have enough challenging work as your skills become higher than what your work requires; or you find yourself in a place where you cannot achieve your goals or live your most important values.

- First, the easiest way forward is to find out whether you can change something within your current position. Ask your manager for more challenging work, or volunteer for a company project. You might also want to train others in what you are doing, be it junior members of the team or people from other teams. In my own experience, this has often been easily achievable and always added great value for everyone. And when the person delivered more value in the same position, typically, their salary also went up.

Sometimes it also helps to be clear about what you really like about your work and what you like less. Recognizing what exactly you like helps you enjoy those moments more and work through what you did not like more quickly. Typically, the people I have seen who were able to do this were also much more inspired by their work and took more pride in their job. However, if you are generally overqualified for the work you are doing or become so over time, or if you feel generally unhappy about your job situation, you should try to change positions.

- Second, you can look for a new position in line with what you have done so far, a next natural move. Obviously, you should try to find something in line with your goals. If you cannot find a natural next step in the short term, do not just wait for an opening to come up, but keep growing. You might further some useful skills you have not mastered yet, such as communication skills, or learn something new.

- Third, you can make a career change in line with newly found insights about your goals, values, or interests. You may also do this if your work is made redundant by technology. This requires courage and effort and may take some time. If you are unhappy with your career so far, you need to think back on how you have chosen your career, whether you have chosen it consciously or more by chance, potentially driven by others' recommendations, by thoughts about money or prestige. Then, the process is the same as for choosing a career: Find something you love to do and can do well that makes an important contribution to others and ultimately to your company. Think hard about how you can manage to become so good at it that you add value and then also receive financial reward. Two useful books that can help you change your career are *I Could Do Anything If Only I Knew What It Was* by Barbara Sher (1994) and *Working Identity* by Herminia Ibarra (2003).

For all these possibilities, when asking yourself whether or not to move forward, or when deciding between various options you could pursue, listen to your feelings. You always should go where you feel the most inner joy. That is your personal path. Positions you feel forced into or that you are not excited about will lead you astray, making your path more winding. Doing them is not impossible, but chances are that they will not fulfill you and that your work is serving someone else's goals. Do not sacrifice anything truly important for your career, be it an important relationship, your core values, or your health. A really great career makes you feel fulfilled in all areas of life.

No one will live without occasional stress, and some positions require you to almost sell your soul to be able to do them, as they require long hours and deep concentration. However, if these conditions are only temporary and part of your long-term plan, and if you are aware of what you are getting into, going through the difficulty can still generate great satisfaction. There is a high correlation between big accomplishments and big challenges. However, you must be aware that you should not push too hard, as above a certain point, people start burning out. They do not get enough sleep because of stress, they lose more energy than they can regenerate, and it devolves into an unsustainable work mode.

On the other end, staying in a job you do not enjoy just to pay the bills may not work in the long run either. If you are dissatisfied at work, you will not have the energy and the will to do what is necessary to develop yourself and you may become outdated. With that, your job will no longer be as secure as you initially thought.

Who gets promoted

I have seen so many cases where people wanting to move further in their career were not promoted or could not get the next coveted position. Although each case is individual, most came down to a few common causes.

- People think that simply being in a position for a certain amount of time naturally entitles them to a promotion or at least a raise. However, you must understand one thing, maybe the most important thing, regarding promotions. It is that there is a direct correlation between value and financial rewards. It may sound simple, but in my experience, most people do not realize it: If you want to earn more money, you need to figure out *how to create more value.* This is true no matter what level you are already at. You can create more value by developing more expertise, or learning new skills, or finding ways to increase productivity, or by making a bigger impact on other people's lives. You somehow need to contribute in a higher way. Simply said, you will not receive more financial rewards unless you become more and deliver more value. Concentrating on the value you contribute will bring you more wealth than simply concentrating on making money.

• The people deciding your promotion do not know about your value. In corporations, these people usually go beyond just your supervisor, and they all need to know about your value. Many people do not understand how promotions take place in their company. Depending on the level in the hierarchy, there are typically yearly meetings where potential promotions are discussed among your manager's peers, their manager, and people from the human resources department. There are formal lists in which potential candidates are listed by position. If your visibility is low with these managers and your manager does not think to bring your name up for whatever reason, you will not be part of these considerations. Whenever a position opens up, this list is the first thing management consults for names. If you hear about the open position and only then bring in your name, you might have lower chances of getting the position.

In fact, some people spend time doing great work and building their skills, but not enough time building relationships. If you do not have exposure to important decision makers who will promote you, your chances for a promotion are lower than someone who has more visibility. The easiest way to get visibility is by demonstrating your main skills and strengths, for example, using your good strategic thinking or superior analysis skills to give helpful feedback, or contributing to a project, or hosting a lunch presentation to discuss a certain topic to showcase your clear communication skills.

Also, when you have done something extra, you should talk about it with others. A former manager always reminded me, "Do good and then talk about it," meaning that I made sure my hard work and accomplishments became known in the wider community. But of course, you should start by telling your manager how much extra you did, as in most cases, they can use this information for themselves. Make sure you keep a list of your accomplishments, so you have them ready when asked or when you bring up the matter of a promotion with your manager. Of course, having a mentor, or even better a sponsor, who facilitates your promotion helps greatly in this respect.

- People do not communicate their wishes. If you know the next position you would like to have or want to develop in a specific direction, you need to make sure your manager knows. Best is to discuss this in a personal development session that many corporations have as a regular process. At the same time, ask what it would take for you to get there—what skills you need to develop, what experiences you need to seek out. In the end, be prepared for your wishes to come true. If you have asked to be transferred abroad, be ready to go there when the time comes.

  Also, dare to ask if a specific opportunity suddenly opens up, such as a position which opens up. If you have discussed your wishes with your manager, he or she will not even be astonished that you are volunteering your name for this opportunity. Sometimes, they may even wait for you to come up with the proposal yourself.

- People are constantly thinking about their next job instead of delivering in their current role. This is especially annoying for managers. Instead of over-networking and looking out for the next opportunity, these people should do their work as well as they possibly can and occasionally should even deliver something extra. Only by exceeding expectations will your career move fast. I always say, your performance in your current job is the application for your next one.

- People do not take enough initiative. *Just working extra hours to get things done is not sufficient for getting a promotion.* Working steadily and spotting problems is good, but is not enough either. You need to go the extra step to propose solutions for problems, or at least proposals for how to find solutions. With that, you show that you have problem-solving abilities and that you care about the company's success. Especially if you aspire to advance vertically, you need to show leadership capabilities in your current position and demonstrate interest in the company beyond your own work responsibility.

- People are not team players. The higher up in the hierarchy, the more important it is that you work well with others. Being kind to others always helps, as it will help you to get what you need from other people, and you will have more friends and fewer enemies. Some people lack listening skills to be good team players. Or they are not easy to work with, as they are "high maintenance," meaning they want to have everything spelled out for them and check back more often than necessary.

- People lack professionalism. Lacking professionalism means talking negatively about the company, management, colleagues, customers, or others. It could also mean sharing confidential information with unauthorized people, and general office gossiping. This is a sad case for a manager. The employee can have everything, go the extra mile, have good ideas, and be well known, but lacking professionalism overtakes all of that. And it is likely the employee does not understand the criticism coming at them in this respect, and hence it is difficult if not impossible to overcome. Once in a while, unprofessional people are nevertheless promoted, but you can sense that it will be their last promotion.

Especially when you want to be promoted to the next level, talking negatively about everything will not serve you. There are so many issues that a manager needs to resolve that you cannot have people in those roles who are always against everything. I have encountered exceptionally skilled people who were negative about almost everything. It was good to get their critical view from time to time, but it was far too much to hear their complaints all the time. It would have been wiser for these people to select a few important things on which to focus their criticism, rather than bothering with the rest.

Talking negatively behind people's backs is unpleasant at any level of the organization, but the higher up you go, the more intolerable it becomes. It taxes everyone's energy and slows down things. It makes everyone's life much easier if people speak up directly when they have an issue. Sometimes, people need to be made aware that they are actually gossiping or even conspiring instead of addressing the issue at hand. They might have started their career in a toxic environment full of gossip and do not know how to behave differently, so it is difficult for them to understand why this type of behavior does not help them advance. Bringing them into problem-solving mode can help to address the underlying issue. I recommend two simple rules here: First, talk to people rather than about people; and second, if you do say things about a person, say it as if they were present in the same room.

- People lack the necessary soft skills. I have rarely seen employees who wanted a promotion and were not technically qualified enough, but every now and then I have seen people who underestimated the soft skills the next position required. Typically, these were communication skills, leadership skills in the sense of leading without authority, but also diplomacy and negotiation skills.

- People often equate making a career with moving up in the company hierarchy and are too fixated on this being their only next career possibility. The fact is that the closer you get to the top of the pyramid, the fewer positions are available, and the greater the competition for them. However, moving up in the hierarchy may even not be the most fulfilling for these people. In many cases, a lateral move makes more sense. I have also seen cases where people only become ready to step up in the hierarchy after making lateral moves.

If you strive to advance in the corporate hierarchy, you have to ask yourself whether it is something you really want. In any case, you have to manage your energy well in order not to lose your peace of mind.

You may have noticed that "bad luck in competition" is not included in the above list. Sometimes people are very quick to tell themselves that it was bad luck that they were passed over for a promotion or position. Of course, if there is competition, bad luck can easily affect the outcome, but it is definitely worth taking a closer, honest look to see if it could have been one of the reasons above and not just coincidence. In any case, being passed over for a promotion or not getting the position you wanted always gifts you with an opportunity to learn. I hope my explanations will give you insights and make you take the actions you need to take the next time.

DO YOU WANT A PROMOTION? DELIVER ABOVE EXPECTATION.

I once had a direct report, a manager of several people, who was very keen on getting ahead in his career. He was responsible for an important area, which he managed very well. He was very diligent and reliable. However, because he was constantly thinking about how to advance his career, he spent a sizeable amount of time strategizing, meeting with people, and networking. As a result, he did not have much mental capacity left over to do any additional work or advance his current team. He only fulfilled his normal job description, which is usually not enough to earn a promotion.

For a promotion, you typically need a few people outside your direct work group to support you. Since he did not produce new work like interesting reports or new initiatives in his field, he did not make much of an impression on those outside of my group. Due to his lack of focus, he failed to show what he was actually capable of and was therefore not the number-one candidate of choice for my colleagues.

DO YOU WANT A PROMOTION? DON'T HIDE YOUR WORK.

Another example comes from an ambitious woman who approached me to discuss having lost a promotion to a colleague whom she felt was less qualified than her. She was a mother of two children and therefore had to manage her time particularly well. She was incredibly organized, always focused, and did exceptional work. Not only was she technically proficient, but she also knew how to get people to work well together. Although she was well respected within her immediate work group, no one outside seemed to know her. She was so focused on delivering good work that she missed building up a network outside of her direct operational network.

Through our conversations, she quickly understood the need to expand her network, especially to people above her level, because they are the ones who will have to agree on her next promotion. She agreed to present her work more often and work on the communication skills needed to do so. Soon after, partly because of my suggestion, she was accepted into a formal, prestigious company program that prepares managers for the next level.

We have seen that the more value we bring, the greater our financial reward will be. Not only do others need to see the value of our work, but we ourselves need to recognize, feel, and ultimately advertise and radiate that value as well. In my career, I have seen many inequities regarding salaries, and much can be explained by people's ability to advocate for themselves. Those who can show their value better than others often had a higher salary, although they might have the same skills to begin with. In my view, this is an important reason why women often earn less than men for the same work. They tend to put less effort into projecting a good image to others and are often, by upbringing, more modest, probably less self-confident, and against showing off. In other words, men tend to overvalue while women tend to undervalue their knowhow, abilities, and contribution. For an interesting book about these particular issues, read *Brag* by Peggy Klaus (2003).

HOLD YOUR VALUE HIGH

I once organized a party for my project team to celebrate the completion of a stressful, large, multi-year project. It was a casual night of bowling with lots of good food. Everyone was either playing, drinking beer, or eating at standing tables. At one point, I listened in on a conversation between a team member on the project and my manager, who had also joined the party. The team member was explaining his role in this important project. He spoke vividly and very passionately about the project and went into great detail about his specific topic, which was improving data quality. The day after the party, my manager mentioned that listening to the man, one could get the impression that he had one of the most important jobs in the entire company. And it was a meaningful job, but clearly far from being one of the most important ones in the company. Since this person thought very highly of his job and expressed great value in it, others who also heard the conversation were likely to think highly of his job too. And I would not be surprised if, as a result, he was compensated generously, certainly more so than someone who was not so passionate and did not think so highly about his own value.

Being passionate about your work and thinking highly of it is the absolute right thing to do. It will bring you financial rewards and happiness at the same time.

Career pitfalls

In the beginning of your career, you will have managers and mentors who will look after your career and will help you along in your work life. They support you and invest in you, as they rightly expect to get good work from you. After some years, you probably are at a high enough level, in terms of salary and specialized expertise, where it is more difficult to change positions. You may have become a threat to the people above you, or your manager may want to keep you as long as possible at your position because you do it so well. Or, if you have stayed a long time in one role, you might not be aware that your skills have slowly gotten outdated, or you got too comfortable and relaxed. In any case, you may not realize that unlike in the past, no one is actively promoting and truly investing in your development anymore. To avoid any of these unfavorable situations, I recommend getting a mentor who helps you regularly assess your situation, or even better a sponsor who actively helps you when looking for a next job. In any case, do not passively wait for a day or an opportunity that will not come.

There are also career pitfalls you might face if you are at the beginning of your career. These are not obvious either. One pitfall is not daring to think big enough, doubting yourself, or being afraid of your own greatness. Not knowing what you want also falls into this category of holding yourself back from fulfilling your potential. Aiming for security in a job may not be the safest approach overall. Going for money first may limit your earning potential at a later stage. Waiting for the right opportunity may take away the chance to gain experience. Meandering because you do not know what you really want may use up your entire work lifetime. To avoid all these pitfalls, knowing what you want and having a direction, a North Star to guide you, may help greatly to find your career path.

Another pitfall I have seen particularly with women is planning too far in advance for the time when they will eventually have children. Some do not go for promotions because they feel it is unfair towards the company if they were to then leave their positions to stay with the children for a while. I have always said that it does not matter for me as a manager whether a person leaves my team or even the company for another position or if a woman takes maternity leave. In both cases, I need a solution for the work that needs to be done. Therefore, I highly recommend going for whatever career path you feel worthwhile for yourself, independent of your plans to stay home with your children or not. The further you can advance your career before having children, the better. Who knows if your plans for having children will pan out exactly as you anticipated? There is enough time to deal with the matter when it comes.

Staying relevant

With the rapid advancements in technology and the acceleration of progress as a result, staying relevant in your work environment is paramount. Staying relevant means not only staying up to date in your field of work and improving your technical skills, but also getting new ideas, cultivating your network, and expanding your soft skills, such as communication and leadership.

To stay relevant for yourself, you also need to work on a contingency plan. This means knowing what to do if your work environment changes in such a way that you no longer want to stay there. To expose yourself to more experiences and possibilities, it makes sense to take part in *company projects*. If you are not asked by your manager, you should suggest it. In addition to enlarging your network and expanding your comfort zone, it will also heighten your visibility. Overall, it is a good way to expose yourself to other fields that could interest you and expand your thinking of what you could possibly do next.

In order to stay relevant, I suggest working with mentors. These are people from outside your close work environment, but who know about the work environment you are in. It is important that they are independent enough to provide objective input. Often, these are people from within the same company and they offer their mentorship for free. They typically answer questions you might have, give advice, provide their knowledge and support. Some companies have formal mentorship programs, but it is best to do it informally, as you can then work with the mentor of your choice.

Start the relationship by bringing your potential mentor a question or problem you would like to solve. If they give you good advice, you may ask for a second meeting in a few days or weeks. You do not have to ask a person to officially become your mentor in your first meeting; it suffices to ask whether you can ask them a question or discuss a problem. A mentorship often evolves over time. And of course, it is important that you trust the person.

It is not always the case that the mentor is older or more senior than the mentee. People talk about reverse mentoring, when the mentor is very young and gives advice, for instance, about new technologies. Most important is that the mentor is more experienced and that the mentee can learn from this experience.

Unlike a sponsor, a mentor usually will not help you find a new job. A sponsor, much like a mentor, is someone who gives advice and feedback, especially regarding the next steps in your career, your career vision and how to grow professionally and personally. The sponsor, however, goes further and advocates for you directly because he or she believes in you and your potential. Usually, a sponsor is a senior-level executive with good connections. Finding a sponsor is not as easy as finding a mentor. You need to first convince the person that you are worthy of promotion and that they should work to help you get it. Typically, a sponsor is someone who sees you perform in your job, such as your manager or other more senior people. Occasionally, a mentor can become a sponsor when enough trust has been built in the person.

GETTING A MENTOR

Early in my own career, my manager asked me whether I would like to have a mentor, because as a woman I would probably face difficulties in advancing my career to my wishes. That was a long time ago, and I politely replied that I would not have the time for a mentor, but might consider it for later. In fact, it quite upset me that my manager thought I should have a mentor when none of my male colleagues did. Hence, I refused something that could have been very beneficial to me. Luckily, I had sponsors at the time who did help me advance. It was not until later in my career that I realized the benefit of mentorships and other organized networking exchanges with more experienced professionals.

Of course, men and women alike should seek advice from experienced people in order to develop constantly. The higher you want to go in the corporate hierarchy, the more important it is that you get this type of help, and not from one mentor only.

Generally, you do not have to agree with your mentors, nor necessarily follow the advice they give you. The main thing is to get their take on things, which in turn can change your view and perspective.

Sometimes, people are afraid to ask someone for advice for free, but typically, people love to make a positive difference in someone's life, and, as we discussed earlier, the act of giving is a gift for the giver. Hence, you should not feel bad about asking for someone's time. However, whenever you work with a mentor, you need to make sure you come prepared and follow up with whatever you have discussed during your meetings. Ask yourself whether you can give back any insights of your own.

SEE MENTORING AS A GIFT

A female top manager who was new in her job once complained to me that she was inundated with requests from young women to become their mentor. In the beginning, she always said yes and limited meetings to four times in four months so she could handle all the requests. However, she stopped accepting new mentees because she became frustrated with the young women either canceling meetings on short notice or not following through with the agreed-upon work. If you have ever seen the crowded calendar of a top executive, you know what it means for them to take time to do something like talk with a mentee. It is an incredible gift for a mentee and should be treated responsibly.

Generally, staying relevant is easy if you like your work. If that is the case, putting in the effort needed to become an expert in your field and learning other relevant skills comes naturally. Hence, you should look out for work you like and drive your own career using joy and excitement as your guide. Do not wait for someone to direct it for you and do not wait for approval from anyone. Become a leader in your own right and take charge of your career.

Summary

- A career is the series of jobs you do throughout your life. As such, literally everyone who works makes a career.

- A particularly good career is one that is driven by growth—that is, growth in knowledge and responsibility as well as personal growth. A successful career leads you into abundance, meaning wealth and money, good health, good relationships, and good levels of self-confidence.

- Choosing a career is finding something that genuinely interests you so much that you love to learn and gain experience in it. Consciously moving forward helps you to stay in the direction of your goals.

- When you feel stuck in a career, the easiest way to change things up is to search for other challenges within your current position. Or you can look for a new position in line with what you have done so far or in line with your goals. Or the next step may be a career change in line with newly found insights about your goals, values, or interests, or if technology has made your work redundant.

- There are various reasons for not getting the promotion or next step you aspired to, ranging from lacking exposure with key decision makers to having a wrong sense of entitlement, lacking skills, or even lacking professionalism.

- Staying relevant means expanding technical and soft skills, getting new ideas, and investing into your network. It also means having a contingency plan in case you want or need to change jobs quickly.

- Having mentors can ease your way throughout your career. Mentors answer questions you might have, give advice, and provide their knowledge and support. They are not from your direct work environment but will be close enough to understand your specific issues.

Exercises

1. Reflect on your career so far. Have you consciously chosen it, or did one thing lead you to the next? Have you thought "big" about what you want? Have you had setbacks where you were not promoted or not offered the job you wanted? What was the reason, in your opinion? Hold it against the above-described reasons. Can you see parallels?

   Are you happy where you are today? Is there an element of growth in your current position? What do you still want to learn in your current position? Would you like to make changes? What would thinking "big" mean for you at the moment?

2. Do you have enough exposure? How many people outside of those you work with every day know about your work? If you want to increase your visibility, what are some ways you could do that? Where could you present your good work? How could you show your value to others, in particular to your manager and his or her peers?

3. Reflect on whether you can provide more value in your current work. For one week, try to contribute more to everyone around you. Do not worry about "what's in it for me." Just deliver more to your manager, to your colleagues, to your direct reports, to your customers. Go the extra mile and aim to delight everyone you work with. During the week, notice how it feels and, afterwards, decide whether you want to continue delivering more value.

4. Think about who you consider a mentor, currently or in the past. Think about what you learned from these people. Have they brought you new contacts? Have they assisted you in problem-solving? What

insights have they received from you? Reflect on whether you can get even more out of these relationships.

Also consider who would be a good mentor for you going forward. Several people may come to mind. Get in contact with them and prepare a set of questions for each. These could be about your personal development, about networking, or about how to solve a particular problem at work. After the meeting, send a thank-you message that very briefly summarizes your meeting, possibly with a list of next steps on your end. Never forget to report back within the agreed time span.

In case you find the exchange trustworthy, constructive, and worthwhile to pursue, in a few weeks or months, ask for a next meeting. Even if you have no further follow-up planned, you can still seek a mentor's advice on what is going on for you at that moment.

Your next career move

If your dreams don't scare you, they are too small.
—Richard Branson

Ideally, your next position will be fully in line with your goals. It should bring you towards your goals and give you opportunities to learn and grow. If you are feeling stuck in a role because you lack support or you are not able to learn any more, or you are not in agreement with the workplace culture, or you are not treated well by your manager, or you generally see no future at your current workplace, then it is time to start looking for a next job.

At the start of every new job hunt, you must check whether the new job is in line with your values and strengths. Just remember, the more you can apply your strengths in your work, the more fulfilled you will be. A job where you can fully live your strengths comes close to being vocational.

The better you can live your values, the more comfortable and confident you will be in your work.

Selecting the right job

You may have several job opportunities to choose from, including the option to stay in your current role. In any big decision like this, you should always listen to your feelings after rationally weighing the offers. Our intuition, which often speaks through our feelings, is often more accurate than rational comparisons because it can incorporate more information than our brain can logically process. This additional information comes from our subconscious mind and beyond. Do you feel joy or excitement when you think about the new job? If so, then it is certainly good and the right thing for you right now. If you are undecided, it is best to sleep on it for a night and in the morning, before you get up, indeed before you even move, ask yourself what you think of the various options.

When you apply for a position, try to find out as much as you can about the job and the company. You probably even know people at that company who can answer questions you might have. They may not be able to tell you everything because of confidentiality, but any information they do give you will help you decide if you really want to apply for the position. If you decide to do so, make sure that the words in your CV or resume and application letter match the words in the job description, because nowadays companies use algorithms to screen applications for possible matches. Only later does the hiring manager see a selection of applications. Even better, if you know someone in the company or even on the team you are applying for, ask if they are willing to refer you to the hiring manager. Then the chances are higher that you will be invited for an interview.

Be aware that more often than one would think, jobs are posted publicly only for process reasons to comply with internal rules and the new position holder is already almost decided upon. Hence, not being chosen in such a case has nothing to do with the quality of your CV. However, probably no one will tell you that this was the true reason for the rejection.

In case you have not been invited for an interview or later offered the position, it might well be that it was not the right job for you anyhow. Keep looking and be clear about what you ideally would like to do in your next position. It is always good to discuss your wishes with some trusted people you respect, be it a mentor or a friend in the business. They will give you an outside view and might advance your thinking. Do not get demotivated; try again for another job. Depending on how well people know your work at your company, chances are high that you will be offered your next job anyhow.

Acing an interview

When you are invited to interview, be it in person or via phone, you need to prepare thoroughly. First, you should research what the company, department, or group you are applying for does. Think about what challenges they may face and how your background could help solve them. The best thing to do is have a vision of the position you are applying for. Go beyond the company's homepage and read any blog posts or reports they may have published on their work. For yourself, be clear why you would like to do this next job and how it helps you on your way forward. Also, formulate some questions that you were not able to find answers for in commonly available information about the company. Be prepared to have some specific questions in case you are prompted to ask.

Also, prepare answers for some obvious questions that human resources people or hiring managers like to ask, such as "Why should we hire you?" or "Why do you fit this role?" and "Can you tell us about yourself and your experience?" In any case, be prepared to answer questions about your CV and any gaps in your employment history. The more you can link your answers back to your personal goals and values, the easier it is to convince someone of the value of your prior experiences.

Typically, you will be asked interview questions that test your technical skills and your behavioral skills, like your ability to work in teams, leadership qualities, communication style, problem-solving abilities, conflict management and ability to cope with failure, and that probably examine your personality type. They will likely be openly formulated: "Can you tell me about yourself?" "What is your work style?" "How do you handle stress and pressure?" "What are your strengths and weaknesses?" "What motivates you?" The best way to prepare is to rehearse answers for such questions in advance, including any specific examples or stories you want to bring up. In case you do not know the exact answer for a particular technical question, you can say so and additionally give your best guess, or describe how you would approach the matter, what line of reasoning you would follow to work the question out as much as you can.

Also, when preparing for the interview, try to intuitively find out what qualities the interviewer considers important. To do this, close your eyes, ask yourself this question silently, and listen for any answers that come up. Also prepare for how you might mention these qualities in the interview.

During the interview, you need to be aware that the first few minutes are of utmost importance. If you can connect with your interviewer and find some *common ground*, you considerably raise the chances of the interview running smoothly. Common ground can be, for instance, people you both know, same prior employer, same alma mater, or if you are from another country or culture, maybe they have visited your homeland. You may want to prepare for this before the interview. In case you cannot find anything to connect on, which I doubt, you could *compliment* something about them or the space, perhaps a painting on the wall or the view from the office.

Having a good executive presence is also important. You must exude that you feel capable of performing the job. Good eye contact and smiling shows that you have things under control. Do not focus on trying to make a good personal impression; rather, show that you care about the work you will be doing.

Just remind yourself that an interview is a two-way street, meaning that the hiring manager is evaluating whether you are a fit, but you also are checking out whether the company or the future manager is a good fit for you. Allow this thought to give you the necessary self-confidence to be your own best advocate.

At the end of the interview, ask whether the interviewer has any doubt that you can fit the role. This gives you the chance to address any potential reservations.

After the interview, make sure you go back to each interviewer and particularly the hiring manager within the next day or two. You can write a short email saying how much you enjoyed the interview and state your gratitude and interest. This is very important if you really want to make sure you get the offer. Explain why you think the job fits you and why you want it dearly.

Above all, the most important part of an interview is your *mental attitude*. The outcome of the interview is dependent on what you think about it. If you are afraid that you might not be good enough for the job, it might well be that the interviewers think the same even if you did not mention your reservations. However proficient your answers may be, if they are not delivered convincingly, they have no real effect. So while preparing the content of your answers is important, mental preparation is even more key.

If you are worried about finding a job, for example because you are coming back from a long maternity leave, you need to prepare yourself well, especially mentally, to be able to appear confident. Reminding yourself of your values combined with affirmations and visualizations may help greatly. Remember, it is all what we think about.

For your next career move, dream big so that you move forward on your path and can fulfill your potential. Always pay attention to joy. Notice when you feel joy in your current work. It will guide you to your next position. Likewise, when deciding on your next career move, perhaps having to choose between multiple offers, make joy and excitement the deciding factors. Discuss your next step with people who understand your industry, profession, or work content. Discussing your options with close relatives or friends who know you but not your work environment can be less helpful, because they will not be able to fully judge the situation. If you let joy and excitement guide you, you can be sure that you are walking on the best path for your life.

Summary

- Your next position ideally is in line with your goals, values, and strengths. The more aligned they are, the more comfortable and confident you will be in your work and the more you will be able to grow.

- When deciding between several options, listen to your intuition, which often speaks through your emotions. It is more accurate than rational thinking for such decisions because it incorporates more information, including from the subconscious mind. If something brings you joy or excitement, then it is the right thing for you.

- The right preparation for a job interview is key. Next to the obvious preparation of researching the position and company and preparing answers to potential technical and behavioral questions, be clear on why you would like to do this next job and how it would help you on your way forward.

- During the interview, having a good executive presence is important for giving people the sense that you are capable of performing the job. Your mental attitude about getting the job is everything.

Exercises

1. Do you have a contingency plan if you should need to leave your current position? Would you know what to do next to find a new position if unforeseen circumstances were to force you out of your current role? Think about what your next position could be. Would you need to widen your network to get there? Would you need to broaden your skills? Think through a few scenarios and decide what you want to do to further prepare for the future.

2. Do you have an up-to-date CV? It is worthwhile to have a CV ready in case someone suggests you apply for a job or if an interesting opportunity comes across your radar. Make sure you note your specific achievements by position, rather than simply listing job title and tasks.

On making yourself visible

If your presence makes no difference, neither will your absence.

—Anonymous

We saw earlier that having exposure within a company is important for getting promoted, because if you are not known outside of your team, even if your manager suggests you being promoted, chances are that it will go to someone else who is better known. Even worse, if you do not have enough exposure and your manager does not raise the idea to promote you, you will not be in the running at all. However, if you are known to your manager's peers, they may put your name on the list of potential candidates for important positions. It is not so much your technical knowledge that determines your chances, nor your quality of work or how well you work with others; it is simply a question of whether you are *known by the decision makers*. Hence, you need to make yourself known. The most direct way you can do this is to make yourself visible and speak up. We will talk about this and other possibilities further down.

There are also other reasons for making yourself visible. Speaking up brings you into discussion with others. You will learn more quickly and easily and become better in your job, and you can also more directly influence the work and potentially implement your ideas. This itself brings you into an achieving mood which, as we saw earlier, is an important factor for happiness.

Another often-overlooked reason for improving your visibility is that you owe it to yourself to be seen. I saw so many knowledgeable people who did not dare to open their mouth for fear that they would say something wrong or undiplomatic, or because they were over-talked by others. Overcoming this fear is something that happens primarily through practice. In less common instances, but more likely with older employees, people feel it is not worth the effort because no one acted on their advice when they spoke up previously. In such cases, it helps to be honest with yourself and to reflect on whether it is that others did not listen or that you should work on your influencing or communication skills.

Either way, choosing not to shine and express yourself is equal to not valuing your skills and ideas. It goes as far as not valuing yourself, which is a true pity. Unfortunately, no one talks about this. You were hired for your technical skills, your personality, and your potential. Unless you have an outward-facing role, most probably it is not written in your job description to make yourself visible. But visibility differentiates you over time from someone who just has great technical and personal skills and makes you someone that everyone *knows* has great technical and personal skills. Those who may have fewer skills but are otherwise recognized have a better chance of being promoted and getting the next job they desire.

If you want to be promoted and advance according to your wishes, I cannot stress enough that you must make yourself visible. Do not wait to be discovered.

STANDING OUT

I know a very successful woman who, after university, started her career in a large department of a large company, being just one among many eager employees. After only a year, she was promoted, and no one could believe how quickly it happened. Her strategy was to be always early for meetings, making sure she had a place at the table opposite the department head. Then she volunteered to take on extra work and asked questions at every meeting, often having thought about them in advance. She said that she always wore jackets in red or another bright color so that after a few meetings, everyone knew her. In addition to all of this, she delivered quality work and made herself indispensable in the department. No wonder everyone wanted her on their team!

Making yourself visible is not the first lesson from the above example; the lesson is actually about something more basic. It is about being part of the discussion, meaning sitting at the table at all. Whenever your work gets presented somewhere, make sure that you are present and get involved, be it as the presenter, or short of that, the person who can field detailed questions. Your manager may be the one to present complex matters to other people;

however, that is not a reason to leave you out. In this common case, ask to be there for learning reasons, so to say, to understand how to present and discuss your work adequately, or at least ask to present your work in front of your own team.

Making yourself heard

To make yourself visible, communication is key, whether written or verbal. If you can express yourself well and in a way that is appropriate for the target audience, you will succeed in making yourself heard. Investing in your communication skills always pays out. Do not only get theoretical knowhow, but practice often. The earlier in your career you dare to express yourself by sharing your opinions in writing or orally, the earlier you become part of discussions, the more you can practice without being afraid of saying something wrong or inapt.

Hence, my advice is simple: If you are not doing it yet, start today with making yourself heard. It will pay out greatly. In case you are already in a leadership position, or you want to grow into one, good communication skills paired with a persuasive presence are indispensable for your success. In any leadership position, people expect you to speak up and say your opinion.

Now, speaking up in a meeting is not everyone's favorite, particularly if you are an introverted person, and it was not mine in certain constellations during the whole of my career. However, you can learn to do it and even enjoy it.

DARING TO SPEAK UP

Early in my own career, I once attended a functional company conference where over a hundred employees from all over the world came together to listen to talks and discuss relevant topics. I was eager to participate and express my opinion. However, I found it incredibly difficult to come up with a meaningful comment or question at the right time. Every time I had an idea of what I wanted to say, the moment to contribute seemed to have already passed. Not to mention, stage fright kept me from speaking up even when the moment was right. But when I finally dared to say something, it felt extremely good afterwards. I guess it was the combination of meaningful contribution and belonging that sparked my happiness.

A good way to start speaking up and being part of the conversation is in fact to make comments or ask questions. If you are nervous about speaking up, prepare comments or questions before the meeting, or write them down during the meeting to formulate them on paper before voicing them. The more inexperienced you are in speaking up, the more you need to prepare to bring your points across in a confident, clear, and concise manner. However, do not speak up to show off or diminish someone's work. Rather, try to contribute by reinforcing or stating an aspect that has not been mentioned before. Also consider that some things may be better shared in a personal conversation after the meeting.

Of course, if you are brand new to the company or to your role, it sometimes does not make sense to say something, as you might not be able to contribute meaningfully just yet. However, you should not miss the point where you transform from a learner to a leader. The more knowledgeable you become, the more people expect you to share your opinion and meaningfully contribute to a discussion. If you are not speaking up when people expect you to give your opinion, then you risk being perceived as not confident, lacking initiative, or being uninterested in the matter and, even worse, in the company itself.

If you are not a complete newcomer, make it a habit to say at least one thing in every meeting you attend. The more you practice, the more you will feel at ease going forward. Again, the easiest point of entry is asking an insightful question. For that, keeping a list of good questions you heard people ask in prior meetings is a nice way to have a starting point for your own. Also, force yourself to have an opinion, whether or not you state it aloud. This will make you feel part of the whole, like you have impact, and give you a sense of belonging.

When it comes to asking questions, people often say that there is no such thing as a stupid question. But in my opinion, this is not true. There are definitely unhelpful questions you can pose in a discussion. Unhelpful questions are those that disturb the flow of a discussion or particularly those which you could answer yourself with a tiny bit of your own thinking. So when you ask a question, make sure it moves the discussion forward in a meaningful way.

So far, we have talked about making comments or posing questions in meetings. The next step is chiming into discussions. Depending on the participants, this can be more difficult, in particular, if you are early in your career and the group usually comprises senior people. However, someone else's position should not prevent you from saying anything.

Now, contributing meaningfully to a good discussion is a challenge in itself. Often, you have people who love to hear themselves talk, making it difficult for others to chime in. These people have no problem with speaking up at all. Ideally, they would say their opinion once and then listen to the arguments of others. However, this is only the case if you have a good discussion moderator. In case you have difficulty speaking at the right time and others have already brought up all your arguments before you could open your mouth, next time try to speak first.

Often, people who talk a lot want confirmation that they are right and end up starting arguments. As a moderator or even a participant of such a discussion, rather than also playing the game of who's right, remind yourself of the following wisdom: It is always better to be kind than to be right. When you think about it, you realize everyone has their own reality. There is no absolute right because everyone has their own unique perception of reality. Each person's reality depends on their expectations, imagination, past and current states of mind, and many other factors. The more you can accept this, the less you have to quarrel and fight, and the easier it is to come up with joint solutions to bring everyone forward. Hence, if you accept that there is no absolute reality and everyone has their own ideas of the situation, then you can fully focus on solving the problem without fighting over who is right. As with anything you send out, kindness comes back. Kindness evokes kindness and spreads beyond. It not only increases positive perspectives but will save you a lot of time and energy too, as you do not have to argue over being right. Hence, being kind instead of right greatly advances problem-solving.

Another aspect of making yourself heard is speaking up about what you want. If the people around you, in particular your manager, or other decision makers, know what your personal goals are, chances are better that you will get what you want.

VOICING YOUR WISHES

I once hired an employee who told me during the job interview that at some point, he would like to go back to Asia, where he had lived for several years. It didn't need to be a specific city or country. As he made a good impression and had the skills we were looking for, we hired him. He did a terrific job and two years later, another department in the same company offered him a superb job in Asia. As I knew it was his dream to go back to Asia, we let him go, even though he had only been around for two years and we had a large, important project to complete. All it would have taken was a brief phone call to stop his move because it was an internal transfer, but fulfilling someone's dreams was too big a joy and we happily let him go.

Saying what you want, however, requires you to be prepared for it to come true. If you say you would like to work at another place and you get an offer to work at another place, it is difficult to not accept. Obviously, you can say no, but if you do not have a convincing reason why you changed your mind in that moment, you might not be presented with the opportunity a second time.

Making yourself useful

Speaking up in meetings is not the only way to make yourself visible. You might choose other possibilities such as volunteering to be part of company projects, organizing something, or starting an independent project.

Volunteering for company projects almost always pays out one way or another. You may learn about topics different from your current work, or you may learn how other people approach problems, or indeed how other people view your work performance. As company projects are often overseen by senior management, you may be seen by those deciding on your next position or promotion. Another way to volunteer and be seen is to come up with your own proposal of something extra you would like to do, for instance simplifying or documenting a process. Figure out what your manager or even your manager's manager wants to achieve, and you may find an opportunity for an extra project to serve these goals. Other possibilities of volunteering are training new hires, covering for others while they are on vacation, or facilitating team meetings. The more you are seen to add value, the better. The more you contribute to important things, the more you will matter. This all requires, though, that you do your daily job sufficiently well to take on the extra load.

If you get the chance to be part of a project outside your daily work, it makes sense that you show them what your strengths and interests are. It is not about bragging, but just about showing who you are. With that, others can see your unique qualities and skills, and when these are needed at another place, your name might come up for a next position.

Speaking up with confidence

To speak up with confidence is first and foremost a matter of mindset. It starts with accepting who you are and being willing to show that. As we have seen, it does not make sense or benefit anyone to pretend that you would be someone different than who you are. However, the difference here is that you must learn to say something to get exposure to others, in particular with more senior people in your company. Hence, you must trust yourself to speak up.

If you are generally nervous about speaking up, you should remind yourself why you want to do this. And rather than trying to calm yourself down in these moments, think of joy and excitement. Also, visualize yourself the last time you asked a good question or made a meaningful comment. Remember how good this felt. It may also help to think about a person who inspires you.

There is also language that works better to build your confidence. Everything that diminishes you, you must omit. Choosing powerful words can make a big difference. The effects of your words are so strong that you will even act differently after having said something differently. For example, if you have firmly expressed your opinion about a proposal to change something, you will later implement that change more decisively and convincingly, whereas if you had expressed it in uncertain terms, you would hesitate with the implementation. Generally, the more precisely and clearly you can express yourself, the better. Avoiding business jargon and abbreviations helps you to be better understood by others. And when you have to voice a concern, it does not help you any to attack others, blame senior management, or be defensive. Rather, state your concerns calmly and go into a positive problem-solving mode. To learn more about this topic, reference *Speak Up, Show Up, and Stand Out* by Loretta Malandro (2014).

Sometimes, people may not want to speak up because they know their manager does not believe in them. In such cases, they would rather say nothing than risk being criticized. This is a pity, and I recommend considering what Eleanor Roosevelt said: "Remember, no one can make you feel inferior without your consent." In fact, having a manager who does not believe in you even after you have proven yourself is reason enough to leave as soon as possible.

Some of you, even after all this, might still not be convinced that making yourself visible is good for you. You might be an introvert who is naturally quiet or shy. But no one said you need to talk a lot or very loudly; you just need to make sure relevant people know you in the end. In particular, women often lead in an invisible way, as speaking up feels inauthentic to them. Rather, they try to promote themselves one-on-one with the key decision makers. This is not a bad strategy in itself. However, it is more cumbersome and time-consuming to advance in such a way. And when these people are looking to be promoted to more senior levels but are not in the habit of speaking up, they are not as well trained in communicating as the job requires, which makes it more difficult for them to succeed in that role. Wanting to stay invisible has less to do with low self-confidence and much more to do with an environment that is not inclusive. For instance, in a more inclusive and diverse environment that assumes enough women are in higher ranks, it becomes less of a problem for women to dare to speak up. All this to say, I understand why some choose invisibility. However, I do not recommend it.

In the end, being good only for yourself is not good enough. You owe it to yourself to shine. Also, when you are in a leadership position, you owe it to your employees to shine for them. They expect it and they love it. The advice in this chapter also applies to everything that has to do with self-sabotage. For example, you should never downplay the value of your work. Instead, simply say "thank you" when someone compliments you. Do not be too modest or too proud of yourself. Be happy about what you have achieved and who you are. With this mindset, it is easier to let yourself shine. And when you shine, you enable others to shine too—your employees, your peers, your managers. As you can see, it is absolutely worth shining your light, because in the end, so much more comes out for everyone.

Speaking up is the single most important way to get exposure with those people who will later promote you or give you your next job. You owe it to yourself to make yourself visible. Remember, you are such a unique and wonderful human being that it will be a pity if the world does not see you shine.

Summary

- In order to be promoted, it is important to be known by the decision makers. To get the necessary exposure, employees have to make themselves visible by speaking up or contributing outside of their own teams.

- Making yourself visible will not only get you more exposure but will help you learn faster about topics of concern and ways of problem-solving. Also, you owe it to yourself to make yourself visible. Your opinion matters.

- A good way to start speaking up is to make comments or ask questions in meetings. Contributing meaningfully to a discussion is more challenging. To allow for a good discussion, it helps to not insist on being right, but rather to be kind. Kindness brings the focus back onto the matter and greatly speeds up problem-solving.

- Volunteering on company projects can also raise your visibility with senior management who decide on promotions and new job offers. If you participate in a project outside the daily work, show your individual strengths and interests such that others see your unique qualities and skills.

Exercises

1. Do you feel you have enough exposure in your company? Whether you are senior or entry level, you need to be known outside of your team. Does your manager's manager know you? Do your manager's peers know you? Do other more senior people know you? What do you think they know about you, for instance about your personality, your work quality, your goals, your career wishes?

   In case you feel you do not have enough exposure, make a plan for how to increase your visibility. Start slowly with speaking up in meetings, chiming in on a discussion, and presenting your work to a larger audience. Set a time in a few months to reflect on your progress in this regard.

2. For two to three weeks, make a resolution to contribute in each and every meeting. Depending on how much you dare to speak, prepare some comments or questions beforehand, or just speak up if you

think of something to say. Go to each meeting with three points you ideally want to get across. In case you are not invited to meetings that often, respond to emails to share your opinion. After each meeting or correspondence, write down how it felt to speak up. After two to three weeks, reflect on what you have written and decide how you would like to go forward.

3. Before an important presentation, take the time to visualize yourself giving a successful presentation and then leading an engaging discussion after. Imagine how good it feels to contribute and answer everyone's questions. In fact, it does not hurt to do this before every meeting.

4. In order to understand how others experience you, ask some people for their perceptions of you in meetings as a presenter or as a normal participant. Ask them about how they perceive your executive presence. You could ask a mentor who regularly sees you in action, your manager, or a friend at work. You will get interesting insights.

   Reflect on whether you would like to change any of your behavior based on the feedback you receive. If yes, make a plan on what exactly you are going to do and after a while, check back with the people you spoke to and ask their thoughts again.

Chapter 5

LEADERSHIP GUIDANCE

Conscious leadership

Greatness is not a function of circumstance. Greatness . . . is a matter of choice.

—Jim Collins

If you manage or lead a team of people, then this chapter is for you. Up to this point I have described what employees who are part of a corporation can do to master their corporate lives and happily advance on their career paths. However, I am sure you have seen or even experienced the tremendous influence managers can have on their teams, both in a positive or negative way. Especially when the manager's influence is negative or lacking, it is difficult for an employee to live a satisfied life. It can bring down the employees' performance or even their careers. Sometimes one individual does not get along well with the manager, or sometimes the whole team suffers. On the other hand, a good manager who is a positive influence can make a team perform better, allowing all members of a team to flourish and bring their best to work. In this chapter, I will give you insights on how you can achieve this.

Managing people and leading people are not the same thing. Management is about execution, while leadership is about motivation. Sometimes people are either classified as managers, who push and direct people, or leaders, who inspire and encourage people. However, to me, someone who has employees reporting to them is both a manager *and* a leader, while someone who directs a group of employees who do not report to them directly in the hierarchy is just a leader. But not every manager is a good leader, and not every good leader is good at management. The question then becomes what a good manager is and, likewise, what makes a good leader. In this chapter, I will address good leadership but not all the varied skills of management, as that would go beyond the scope of the book.

The need for new leadership styles

Over the past few decades, various trends have emerged in leadership styles. The development of these new leadership styles was a result of the evolution of businesses and even more the needs of people working in these businesses. Whereas decades ago, autocratic and paternalistic leadership styles may have prevailed, in more recent times, democratic and transactional leadership styles have become common. These days, transformational leadership styles are applied more often.

To understand these phases of leadership style, let us look at how companies' focus changed as businesses evolved. When I started my career, *shareholder* centricity was of utmost importance and in every strategic meeting shareholder value was the most-heard expression. After a while, people started to talk about *stakeholder* value, meaning the interests of other parties such as customers and employees, but shareholder value remained the first priority. Already back then, I was wondering why people did not talk more about customers or even employees in their strategies.

However, some years ago, businesses started to put *customers* at the center of their thinking. This made sense as companies struggled to come up with meaningful ways to grow and innovate. Putting the customer at the center helped them to build products customers would need and buy. When companies made the customers their focal point and in every strategic meeting, customer was the most-heard word, I wondered why there was still not more talk about *employees*. After all, without employees, no business is worth anything. These days, many exceptionally successful companies do in fact put employees at the center of their strategic thinking. As Richard Branson, CEO of Virgin Airlines, says, "Clients do not come first. Employees come first. If you take care of your employees, they will take care of the clients."

If you start with the employees and give them what they need, they will bring their best to work, and you will have better teams who invent and create better products and better sales for happier clients and better results and higher profit in the end. You could keep moving inward: If you put yourself at the center, everyone around you will benefit. If you take care of yourself, you are able to care for others. If you make yourself a priority, you will be developing yourself, you will feel energized, and you will have more to give to others.

In a business context, all this is quite natural. First, you need to make sure you are functioning well. It is not at all selfish or egoistic to put yourself first. Then you can look out for those around you—your employees, your manager, probably your peers too. If they have everything they need to function well, together you will have immense energy, focus, and motivation to look after your business, your clients, and their needs. As a conscious person, you know anyhow that whatever you give will come back to you, including success, which is particularly important in business.

There are also other reasons a leadership style centered on human needs is effective. Just think about the current business environment. It has become more and more complex over the years. Many companies operate with complex matrix structures, global businesses are spread over many locations and time zones, and the systems landscape has become more complicated than ever, with the challenge of maintaining consistent data over complex system architectures. The world has become more interconnected, more global, and more digital. Complexity will continue to increase, as we live in an expanding universe.

The overall problem is in fact twofold. On the one hand, in the outer world, humankind is facing huge challenges with extreme weather, biodiversity loss, infectious diseases, overpopulation, cybersecurity failure, digital inequality, and others. On the other hand, in our inner world, people struggle with their own personalities, self-doubt, work-related stress, or mental health issues such as anxiety or depression.

Considering these issues and the increasingly complex environment, it becomes vitally important that people can work at their best, that they are willing to bring their best to work, and that they work in a way that is sustainable over many years. This most likely is going to happen when people, especially managers, are conscious about their own inner world, what drives them, what makes them feel purposeful, and what makes them happy. Hence, our modern world requires leadership styles that put human needs at their center.

Leadership styles with a future

For some years now, people-centered leadership styles have been propagated under the names of transformational leadership, inclusive leadership, positive leadership, authentic leadership, or conscious leadership. They all have in common that they put people and their development first. Typical elements of all these leadership styles include:

- They encourage cultivating a *high level of self-awareness*, meaning that people know themselves, their beliefs, values, and goals—and work accordingly.

- They create an environment where a *culture of trust and care* prevails. They prioritize consistent and fair treatment of employees, business partners, and all stakeholders. If a leader authentically lives these values, the employees will follow their lead and live them too. This holds true for business partners and all stakeholders too. This sort of trusting environment is good for not only others, but also for the leader's own well-being.

- Great importance is attached to the *growth of individuals*. Continuous development is propagated according to the individuals' needs, in order to fulfill their tasks and objectives in the best possible way. Leaders therefore propose customized approaches to each person. Managers are encouraged to recognize and develop the potential of their employees. This ultimately helps individuals develop to their best and bring the same to their work.

- A high value is placed on *higher purpose*, meaning having a vision and reason for the future. To accomplish this, leaders make the connection between the tasks and values of individual team members to this higher vision and the values of the whole team and organization. Linking people's individual contributions to the company's goals and vision gives purpose and increases individual motivation. This is even more the case if the employees are part of developing the vision.

Additionally, transformational leadership propagates providing an *intellectually stimulating environment* for the employees, where leaders empower the employees to think independently and creatively, to challenge the status quo, and to come up with innovative ideas to transform businesses.

Inclusive leadership emphasizes *diversity and inclusion*, where every person's uniqueness is brought in without bias. Later in this chapter, we will come back to how we can work in an inclusive way and the countless benefits of doing so.

Positive leadership additionally concentrates on *enhancing positive emotions* in order to create a safe place for all employees. Positive emotions change the way the brain works. People are more creative and quicker to problem-solve. They focus on what is feasible rather than what is wrong or considered impossible. Research shows that a positive work environment is more productive, more customer focused, more fun, and certainly healthier than a fear-driven one (Seligman 2011).

In addition to open, honest, and trustful relationships with employees and stakeholders, authentic leadership promotes ethical behavior and *ethical business practices*, which include unbiased decision-making. Authentic leadership is leading with heart and head, meaning having compassion for people and feeling connected to them. For more on authentic leadership, see *Authentic Leadership* by Bill George (2003).

Conscious leaders are deliberate in how they live their lives and interact with others. They want to be themselves. They do not want to pretend in any way, nor to act as though they know everything. They have the courage to admit that they do not have all the right answers. Instead, they ask the right questions. They do not lead with power, but know how to empower their teams. Most importantly, they assume *100 percent responsibility for their lives* and follow through on their commitments. For more on this style of leadership, see *Conscious Leadership* by John Mackey, Steve McIntosh, and Carter Phipps (2020).

With all these leadership styles, positive business results and profitability are considered a logical result of the employees' needs being properly met. However, the consideration of stakeholder value, meaning thinking about the needs of all involved parties, including even the environment and the planet, and *deciding for the "greater good"* is nevertheless a high priority.

With a human-centered leadership style, employees feel psychologically safe and show less resistance to change and therefore quickly implement what needs to be changed. They are more creative and innovative, and therefore they are better able to solve problems and continuously improve their work. Higher employee engagement and motivation leads to better team performance, superior customer service, and ultimately *dramatically higher profits* (Mackey and Sisodia 2014).

What else is conscious leadership?

Going deeper on conscious leadership, being 100 percent responsible for your own life means accepting what is and not blaming others for whatever happens to you. It means taking full control of your results and your relationships with others. It means learning from mistakes instead of just accepting them. It means coming away from feeling like a victim to taking agency. This includes not blaming others or circumstances for your mistakes or disappointments. By being 100 percent responsible and accountable, you are fully conscious about how you act and react.

The precondition to being able to be 100 percent responsible is being conscious about what level of responsibility you currently take. Most people you meet in corporations do not take 100 percent responsibility for themselves. You may know some obvious cases, where people blame everything on circumstances. They are defensive, want to always be right, often talk badly about others behind their backs, and generally are reluctant to take over responsibility and make commitments. These tendencies can become more subtle, though, when you think you are taking on 100 percent responsibility, but you are in fact not. Signs of this include wanting to be absolutely right, having a narrow outlook, or thinking you cannot change anything due to circumstances.

Once you are aware of your current level of responsibility, you can move towards becoming 100 percent responsible. You will be greatly rewarded, as you will allow yourself to be the creator of your own life. You will act and speak differently, show more presence, be more confident, and address difficult situations more directly. You will be more open to change and be fully committed to learning. You will also be more forgiving and more easily let go of things that are no longer relevant.

When you have committed to full responsibility for your own life and well-being, you will start to silently influence others too, just by radiating credibility and good qualities. More than likely, you will actively support your team and others to take full responsibility for their lives too. Then your team will become more conscious, more confident, more skilled, and overall more successful too.

Very importantly, do not be negatively influenced by people who do not take responsibility for themselves. Even if others take 0 percent responsibility, you should not deviate from your 100 percent responsibility principle in order to keep your power. I know this is not an easy task. Sometimes, it would be much easier to mirror the other person and just complain and blame the circumstances too. However, just know that that means giving up your power.

Conscious leadership is keeping humans at the center of your thinking. The more conscious you become about yourself and others, the more you will recognize that people are more connected than we usually think or sometimes want. However, the more you realize this, the more you can use it to benefit everyone. Employees who feel a connection to their manager may work harder. Leaders who feel a connection to their employees treat them more fairly. It is very much human nature to want to be connected, to be part of a greater whole. The more we think we are separated from each other, the more we start fighting and defending our own positions. But the more we think we are connected, the more collaborative our solutions will be, the more we support each other, and the easier it is to create win-win situations for everyone involved.

How leaders can change

The good thing about a human-centered leadership style is that it can be lived by every leader, regardless of what other leaders in the company are doing. Unfortunately, in some companies, leadership development is often not a priority. Leadership style is rather seen as a matter of personality. Hence, there is some uncertainty about what type of leadership is expected from leaders in the company. We have seen that applying human-centered leadership has so many benefits that it would be most effective if everyone would apply it. However, it is not necessary to wait for your company to officially endorse it; you can start applying it today.

What exactly is needed to begin your practice of human-centered leadership? Well, it starts with self-awareness. I touched on this topic earlier in the book, but to be clear, self-awareness means knowing and understanding your own personality and individuality, your own values and beliefs, and your own feelings and desires. It is also about how others see us and how we fit into the world. Usually, people are not trained in being self-aware. Many only start to reflect on themselves when something goes terribly wrong. Short of that, people typically make excuses, get defensive, or continue to blame others for their reactions. With self-awareness, you are able to understand why you react a certain way to external irritants and what you could do to change your behavior. Otherwise, you may unconsciously react in patterns you adopted from others, and you may waste a lot of time on being upset. In that time, you could have already solved the problem. However, it is important that self-awareness does not lead into self-doubt. You can avoid this by being clear and proud about your own values.

Self-awareness also helps you recognize when you are stressed and when the stress is actually too much for you. This will make your business life more sustainable, as you will know how to manage your energy and when you need to make time for rest and recreation, instead of slowly burning out. My advice is to ask yourself from time to time if what you are doing is good for you.

Self-awareness also influences personal development. You know your strengths and how you can apply and further strengthen them. Also, when opportunities come up, you will better know whether or not they fit you well. You will also know your team members' strengths and how to promote them. Hence, you do not have to put your efforts in trying to fix weaknesses, but rather work on supporting everyone's strengths. This will lead your team to flourish.

From a place of self-awareness, it is only a little step further to being aware of your team members, what they know and what they need. You are able to help them develop by providing precise feedback. In turn, they will have trust in you, and you will have their loyalty. And this will be true for every person you interact with, even people beyond your own team. If you know what they really want and need, you will more easily be able to support them, and they will trust and be loyal to you.

FOCUSING ON EMPLOYEES' STRENGTH

I once had a job opening and hired a person internally despite mediocre performance reviews because I saw a lot of potential in her. The work she had to do on my team was not too complicated, so I thought I would give her a chance. Her former supervisor's manager, a peer of mine, told me that they would be glad not to have her on the team anymore because she did not deliver good work. However, once she joined my team, we focused on her strengths and developing them further. Her confidence increased and after a while, she delivered very satisfying results. One day, she volunteered to work on a departmental project and did a tremendous job. She was then able to present the work of the entire team to the company's management. Building on this work, she was even able to co-lead a workshop with my peer. He would never have thought it possible, but focusing on her strengths instead of her weaknesses made it so.

The better you know your team members, the more you are able to help them develop and improve and the more you can empower them. They will then do their jobs better, which will lift up the whole company in the end.

All this requires a leader who can be a *coach*. A coach asks questions rather than providing answers, supports employees rather than judging them. A coach recognizes a person's potential and facilitates their development. A coach creates the right conditions for learning and an environment that motivates people and makes them want to bring their best to work. Being a coach means being able to listen, being open to other standpoints, being empathetic and considering other people's feelings, taking them into account particularly when making decisions that impact everyone.

Applying a human-centered leadership approach means that you will become more honest and human as a leader. You will be accessible and more inclusive because you value and respect people as they are. With that, you will be presented with information and probably opposing viewpoints, which are all the more welcome for coming up with solid solutions. In this mindset, you will be more welcoming to change and better equipped for the challenges of the future.

Research shows that self-aware people are more fulfilled, have better relationships, are more creative and confident, are better communicators and leaders, and that businesses led by self-aware leaders tend to be more profitable (Eurich 2017). However, research also shows that people heavily overestimate their level of self-awareness. A good test of whether you are as self-aware as you think is to collect 360-degree feedback, asking your manager, peers, and team members to assess your self-awareness. Do they come up with the same number as you?

If you wonder what else you can do to become more self-aware, there are the usual suspects like knowing who you are and what you want as well as knowing your values and living them daily, all as discussed earlier in this book. Self-awareness is not so much about introspection and exploring the cause of things but more about realizing what is and then finding ways to go forward.

The outcome will be extraordinary

If you already do or if you decide to apply a human-centered leadership style, you will not only benefit in your business life, but also in your private life. You will take more responsibility for yourself, which does not mean more work, as you might delegate more work or omit doing less important things. You will influence others in a positive way, such that they are able to flourish, be it in their private or business lives. You will feel better connected with yourself and others and therefore will collaborate with excellent rapport. You will be able to build an environment of trust and care, where people can grow and feel fulfilled.

You will realize that considering the interests of all stakeholders, starting with yourself and your employees, will take you farthest. After all, by being more conscious, you will show more integrity, gain more clarity, and will fully engage with your mind, heart, and soul.

Summary

- Prevalent leadership styles evolved over time from autocratic and paternalistic to democratic and transactional leadership styles. These days, human-centered, transformational leadership styles are increasingly applied.

- Human-centered leadership styles are known under the names of transformational, inclusive, positive, authentic, or conscious leadership. They put people and their development at the center.

- Typical elements of human-centered leadership are: high level of self-awareness, culture of trust and care, dedication to the growth of individuals, high value put on higher purpose, making decisions for the "greater good."

- With a human-centered leadership style, the leader is taking care of him- or herself first, because only then can he or she sustainably serve others—employees, managers, and all other stakeholders.

- Conscious leadership is about taking 100 percent responsibility. This means taking full control of your results and relationships with others, learning from mistakes, and being a creator. Less than 100 percent responsibility is feeling like a victim, blaming others or circumstances for your own mistakes or disappointments.

- Becoming a conscious leader means becoming self-aware, being clear about your personality, individuality, values, and beliefs.

- Applying a human-centered leadership style leads to more employee engagement, more innovation, and better business results.

Exercises

1. Do you know people who are conscious leaders? They themselves may not call it that, but you will recognize them as such. Try to spend time with them. It will make you a more conscious leader too. Remember, the people you spend time with affect the way you feel, think, speak, and act.

2. Reflect on your past managers or leaders with whom you have worked, including mentors, colleagues, or peers. Were they influential in your life? Who would you like to work with again? List five qualities that you notice in each of those people. For each quality, note whether it is of a technical nature, such as a skill the person has, or whether it has more to do with the personality and values of that person. You might have qualities from both categories for each person. Look at the sum of all the qualities by category. You may get insights on what you would want to focus on in the future.

3. Next time you notice yourself wanting to be right, making excuses, reacting defensively, avoiding tough conversations, or thinking you cannot change anything due to circumstances, take a step back and find a way to take 100 percent responsibility. Hold yourself accountable.

You could, for instance, look into various options on how you could be more effective, or confront tough conversations, or resolve negative situations rather than tolerating them.

After having taken action, reflect on whether you have reached 100 percent responsibility or whether you need to take more ownership through your thoughts and actions. Also reflect on whether your action was the most efficient resolution, or whether you have room for improvement next time.

4. Take your last 360-degree feedback review or your last performance review and reflect on where your own assessment deviates from your supervisor's or others' assessments of you.

If you have not done any 360-degree feedback yet, you could ask your manager to do one; your company's human resources department will typically have such a tool available. Or you could also come up with a few questions on your own and ask a friendly business colleague to do the exercise, just the two of you. You could include questions about what you stand for, your values, your goals, your behavior in a given situation, your response to failure or mistakes, your impact, or anything else you want to reflect on.

The necessity of inclusion

No one likes to be managed. But everyone longs to be included.

—Sadhguru

If you want to create an environment where employees bring their best to work, there is no doubt about the need for *inclusion*. Inclusion means respecting people's uniqueness in an empathetic way. Also, if you want to create solutions that are relevant for everyone, be it clients, employees, or other stakeholders, then you need *diversity*. And, if you want a fair play for everyone, you need *equality*. It is as simple as that.

Not everyone in the modern workplace has really understood this yet, although these topics are widely addressed in today's corporations. Some companies address these topics primarily to avoid legal charges that could be brought against them if they ignore the problem. Others center their efforts in these areas around moral or ethical reasons. While the issue is a moral one, you do not have to go that far; it is already enough to understand that diversity and inclusion are necessary for economic reasons. If you want an engaged workforce, if you want the best employees, and if you want these employees to bring their best performance to work, there is no way around diversity, inclusion, and equality.

What we want to achieve through diversity and inclusion

Diversity can apply to many things—age, gender, nationality or ethnic origin, religion and belief, and so on. In a corporate context, a major form of needed diversity is diversity in thinking. The more diverse a group's thinking, the more different views and ideas you will get, and the more diverse clientele can be optimally served. Innovation comes more naturally in diverse groups.

In addition, the talent pool of potential employees is larger when you consider a wider, more diverse range of people. A very famous example of this came up a few decades ago when orchestras changed the way they hired musicians. They started doing blind auditions, where the musicians played from behind a curtain. This ensured that only sound counted, not appearance. The result was that orchestras suddenly filled up with women. Given that orchestras up to that point were dominated by men, jurors tended to hire men. By removing one simple bias, the talent pool essentially doubled, the quality level of orchestras has risen, and the process become much fairer for everyone.

For corporations, this shows that if a business is operated by a homogeneous group of people, the fair hiring process can give way to groupthink. People will mostly confirm the leader's view, or those who have arguments against those views will fear bringing them up because of group pressure. It may be that people become overconfident and take too much risk, or that they take too few risks because they do not realize the scope of what is possible or because they lack ideas.

However, diversity alone is not a magic bullet. You can have wonderfully diverse groups, but if the different voices are not being heard, the environment is not inclusive. An inclusive environment is one where people are invited and dare to state their opinion, where everyone is accepted and treated fairly, and where no one feels above or below others. Inclusion goes beyond accepting people as they are. It is wanting people to be who they are. Typically, inclusive leaders create such an environment.

There is yet another reason why we must push for more diversity and inclusion. For centuries, our businesses were led in a masculine way, mostly by men, but also by women. Qualities such as logic, force, objectivity, and competition dominated the decision-making. Contrast this with feminine qualities, such as compassion, creativity, intuition, connection, and healing. All people, both men and women, have masculine and feminine qualities, and living predominantly by one set of qualities, whether it be masculine or feminine, is not fulfilling one's full potential. Hence, men and women are more whole and fulfilled if they can genuinely express qualities from both sides of the spectrum. If we want to live our whole human potential, we need to include both ways of thinking in how we lead our businesses. Balancing these qualities will also balance society. And more importantly, applying all these qualities in business will help us with the incredible challenges we face as a society to live on this planet in a sustainable way.

Inclusion without bias

Given its many benefits, why is not everyone inclusive right away? The previous chapter about networks touched on the human brain's tendency to like what is familiar to it. Therefore, we like to be around people who are like us, and this is why we often resist change. Homophily is a key word here.

Humans are prejudiced against people who are different from or think differently than them. Prejudices can be open or hidden. Open prejudices are known to the person who holds them, while hidden ones are more unconscious biases that the person is unaware of.

To overcome *open* prejudices, it helps to become a more open person, allowing yourself to adjust your ideas, opening yourself to more options, thinking for yourself, not following groupthink, accepting that everyone has their own reality, detaching from the things that are given and taking a more distanced view. It also helps to study your own limiting beliefs, where they come from, whether they are still worth carrying around or whether you want to let them go.

A *hidden* prejudice, often called an *unconscious bias*, is a prejudice we have against something, a person, or a group. However, the difficulty is that we are not aware of it. It is a result of external influences on us, our upbringing, or our environment. Typically, an unconscious bias is subjective, unintentional, and often untrue when viewed objectively. In many cases, unconscious bias is unfair to the group of people it affects and leads to discrimination. An example is when a candidate's gender, name, or interests unconsciously factor into the hiring process.

In the orchestra example I described earlier, the unconscious bias of the jurors could be addressed by the simple and highly effective solution of letting the candidates play behind a curtain. Unfortunately, there are hundreds of other examples of unconscious bias that are not so easily solved.

Unconscious bias can apply to any type of diversity, such as gender, race, country of origin, age, disability, appearance, weight, beauty, height, religion, or other characteristics. It can even lead to being prejudiced against people who think differently than you do. There are many studies on this topic, but often these studies suggest further research as a result. Clearly, the topic is complex.

On the internet, you can find tests, called Implicit Association Tests, to assess your own levels of bias. You can find out the extent to which unconscious thought patterns influence your actions. While Implicit Association Tests themselves are not perfect and have built-in confirmation biases stemming from the order in which the questions are posed, they can still serve to raise your awareness about any unconscious bias.

Unconscious bias is sometimes difficult to uncover, as bias can exist not only in an individual or group of individuals, but even in an entire institution. The latter can be very problematic, as no one within the system sees that there is unfairness, and meanwhile they face more and more missed opportunities.

Inclusion together with diversity brings more differing viewpoints, more creativity, more collaboration, more innovation and, importantly, more engagement of the workforce.

These days, it is fashionable to put diversity and inclusion on the corporate agenda and on various managers' agendas. This is needed and important, as instances of unconscious bias are common, as the following example shows.

UNCONSCIOUS BIAS

Early in my corporate career, I was invited to a prestigious communications training at the head office of my company. When I arrived, I found myself among senior and very senior managers, which made me feel a bit intimidated. One afternoon, we divided into two groups and took part in a relatively long role play about how to communicate in a crisis. I first mainly listened to the conversation. After some time, I thought that the most important factor had not come up yet. When I finally expressed my thoughts, the entire discussion and outcome changed.

It turned out that in the other group, they had a similar discussion, where someone who was rather quiet ultimately changed the outcome. Afterwards, two people from the organizing team who had observed the groups during the exercise debriefed the entire team. Subsequently, the manager of the organizers (who only participated in the summary meeting) went on stage to say a few closing words. He pointed out the importance of listening to younger and quieter people, as they too may have something valuable to say. Then he literally said, "Who would have ever thought that a liftboy from Singapore and a housewife from Switzerland would have the most brilliant ideas?" Of course, I did not find that funny.

Ironically, this was one of the top managers in the entire company, who, by the way, had a team that regularly informed the company about diversity and inclusion. But he obviously did not live the values the team espoused.

These days, many managers have diversity and inclusion as responsibilities. However, I have seen too many of them just pay lip service, associating themselves with the topic, setting up discussion groups and launching action campaigns without following through, and not actually making tough decisions to bring about real change in this respect. I have seen these types of managers mentoring women. They loved giving them advice but were reluctant to take the last steps of sponsoring them and promoting them into bigger roles.

What is needed from leadership

There are basically two ways to become truly inclusive—either *transform people's thinking* to be inclusive, or *build structures* where diversity and inclusive thinking are forced to the surface. The first option requires educating people on their unconscious biases and why diversity is desired. The second does not necessarily require everyone to think inclusively, but only those who decide on processes and policies. The latter is sometimes referred to as *behavioral design*.

It is an almost impossible undertaking to try to convince everyone that diversity and inclusion is desired and much needed. This is because biases typically are unconscious. This means that we are unaware of them; however, they are hardwired in our subconscious mind. Becoming aware of our biases requires a lot of personal work. Some people do not even want to change, as change would require them to reevaluate what they have learned and what they have been taught. Changing their views causes them to fear losing their identity or may go against their values.

However, raising awareness within companies is nevertheless important. Especially those people hiring and promoting people need to be educated about where unconscious bias occurs in everyday work and how it can be counteracted in order to make fair and objective personnel decisions based on suitability and competence, not similarity and groupthink. In general, leaders should be taught how to make objective decisions free of prejudice.

In addition, as is the case with all cultural change, it is a prerequisite that top managers raise their voices and openly commit to diversity, equality,

and inclusion. They not only need to hold themselves but the entire organization accountable. They need to be transparent on the current state of
things and draw a picture of the future they aspire to, be it diversity, hiring
or promotion goals, wage equality, or some other target.

Applying behavioral design in corporations can be much less expensive
and less difficult than de-biasing people. In some cases, changes that happen
almost for free can have a big impact. I personally have experienced measures
that did work well. There are also many books and articles about actions
that have a positive impact on equality. For instance, *What Works: Gender
Equality by Design* by Iris Bohnet (2016) gives good insight backed up with
scientific studies.

The following are measures I have seen or heard directly that work:

- If you want to quickly achieve a critical mass of diversity in a team,
  nothing is as effective as the *introduction of quotas*, where you prescribe
  the desired ratio, for instance of women or people of color, that you
  would like to have in a team. Although quotas have long been frowned
  upon, they are very effective when applied reasonably.

A FAIRER PLAY

When I entered the business world many years ago, there were already
conversations about having an equal distribution of women and men
through all levels in the workforce. There were endless discussions about
why women would face "glass ceilings," meaning that they would be unable
to rise up the corporate hierarchy above certain management levels, even
though they were fully qualified to do so. At some companies' top management levels, which are typically visible to the outside world, satisfactory
gender ratios were achieved over the years. At the levels below, however,
the ratios changed only very slowly or not at all.

In the company I worked for, after many years of trying to promote
women to higher levels, the CEO made the bold decision to introduce
moderate quotas, which he then raised every year. If top managers did

not achieve these quotas in their area of responsibility, they would not get their full bonuses. This led men to fear stagnation in their careers, and there was much talk about "quota women" who were undeservedly promoted. However, the women who were promoted brought so much diverse thinking, fresh air, and increased collaboration into their respective areas of the company that after a few months, no one talked about "quota women" anymore. On the contrary, the vast majority of people agreed that they were in fact excellent choices.

To get the effect of diversity, you need a critical mass of people. Research suggests this is around 30 percent for any minority. To make it a fair change, when introducing quotas, you should also make sure that the majority does not become the minority over time. Hence, some companies started to introduce so-called *symmetric quotas* for women and men. They seem to be better accepted.

As an alternative to strict quotas, some companies request quotas on the number of positions refilled. This may be a much slower way to achieve diversity, though, dependent on team fluctuation.

- Another effective measure is *rethinking promotion criteria,* as demonstrated by the following example.

ADAPTING PROMOTION CRITERIA

A colleague and partner of a major consultancy firm once told me about a selection panel he had sat on for selecting new partners. They had interviewed the candidates beforehand and asked them why they wanted to become partners. One woman in her interview said that she was already doing the work of a partner, hence she felt she should also be named as such. When the panel discussed this woman's candidacy, some people thought she did not seem eager enough to become a partner and the hunger was missing in her. However, in the end, this woman was elected partner, and sometime after, everyone agreed that she was the best addition they could have made.

Not everyone who is capable is eager to move up in the hierarchy at any and all cost. On the contrary, some people have been downright discouraged from moving up through unfair competition, so even though they are highly qualified for the job, they do not seek it. Changing promotion criteria to really bring up the best talent and not the most eager would help in such instances.

Women and men tend to have different beliefs about why they received certain promotions. Whereas men usually believe that they got where they are thanks to their talent, women tend to believe it is their competence, good results, and hard work that helped them advance. Hence, they often concentrate less on networking and self-promotion, which can be interpreted as lack of ambition. Thus, changing promotion criteria and not silently assuming things is a prerequisite for more equality.

- Similar to rethinking promotion criteria, the next measure is *rethinking leadership criteria*. From the examples above, it is clear that women tend to lead differently than men. Although every individual is different, I have lately seen tendencies, especially among younger women leaders, to be more collaborative and less competitive among their teams. Hence, if you want to bring top talent and diverse views into higher ranks of the company, it is important to reformulate what good leadership is to include both male and female attributes. Otherwise, traditional, supposedly objective leadership criteria lead to unconscious anti-selection. In the meantime, luckily, leadership attributes that were fashionable some years ago such as prioritizing work above all else, even before one's own health, and working excessive hours have faded from the scene. A more balanced view of leadership attributes is healthy for companies and for everyone who works there.

- The *use of inclusive language* has been widely studied. Especially in job descriptions, unbiased language can make a difference. Research shows that job descriptions often contain words that have a masculine connotation, even though they explicitly state that both genders are desired as candidates. With that sort of language, such job descriptions are more likely to appeal to men. With a gender-neutral tone, more women would apply. This includes, for instance, replacing words such as "leadership," "driven," "results," and "autonomy" with words like "direction," "motivated," "outcomes," and "freedom."

  It is also important to use inclusive language in internal and external communications and publications. A company's communications department should give out directions on how to formulate texts in gender-neutral language.

- When hiring for an open position, candidate selection should be done, as much as possible, in a "blind" way, meaning *anonymizing application documents* for names, addresses, photos, age, interests in the beginning, as far as up to the first round of in-person or video interviews. Of course, one cannot cancel out everything that a hiring manager could be biased for, but hiding certain factors in the beginning can let the really relevant pieces of information shine.

  If hiring managers insist on making decisions based on gut feeling, then you can assume they hire based on unconscious biases, affinity being the most obvious bias in this case. Without being conscious of biases, we naturally pick people who are like us and have similar skills. Obviously, doing things this way does not bring diversity, but only serves to duplicate us. Preventing this starts by becoming aware of typical biases humans have, and realizing that unbiased hiring brings more diversity and with that better problem-solving and more innovation and profitability to the workplace. However, also do not overcompensate—similarities should not be a criterion to rule out a candidate, but they should not be the deciding factor either.

Also important, when you decide on a candidate as a team, it is recommended that everyone gives his or her opinion about the candidate in writing, such that conformity bias can be ruled out.

- Another measure, which helps to revise biases we have developed through our lives, is to *show role models*.

PRESENTING ROLE MODELS

I once organized a series of presentations by successful women to give younger women role models in the industry. I was not at all sure beforehand whether the series would be a success, but I wanted to provide these younger women something I did not have. When I started my career, there were not many women in higher positions in my industry, my company, and my functional area. And I personally could not identify with the women who were there, because most of them did not seem to know the demands of family life. Anyhow, the series were a huge success and the younger women in attendance were very interested in seeing how these senior women organized their lives and how they had advanced their careers.

When providing role models, you do not necessarily need to showcase the most inspirational people. More important is to have speakers that are genuine and authentic, that do not fear talking about difficulties they faced, and that people can easily relate to. In case you cannot find presenters within your company, invite external people of the respective minority you would like to support for more diversity.

- An important move to achieve for gender diversity is to celebrate and *showcase examples where childcare is more equally split between the parents*. If we get to a place where childcare and family care is not seen to be mainly a woman's issue, we will reach more equality. In my teams, I celebrated each time a young father took several months off to look after a new baby, not always leaving that to the mother. With that in mind, companies are required to be more flexible about maternity and paternity leave, but they will be rewarded with more fulfilled employees. In corporations, we must come to a place where it is equally acceptable for men and women to have the possibility to take part in raising their children without the punishment of stagnating careers.

How to be inclusive

First, I want to clarify that inclusion does not mean listening to and including all opinions at all times. This would certainly not be efficient. Some situations call for a diverse set of opinions; other times, it is not necessary. For instance, to formulate corporate values, strategy, and business goals, or to solve problems or creating new processes or products, diverse views help. However, to complete tasks or advance on predefined goals, you do not need to consult more people than minimally necessary.

The more *diversity in thinking* you have in a team—which is one of the main reasons why we want people of diverse backgrounds—the more inclusive you have to be as a leader. The goal should be to allow for as many different opinions as possible to collectively come up with the best solutions. However, it can be strenuous to listen to all opinions at the table and afterwards to discuss and come up with a joint solution. To have meaningful discussions, as a leader you have to value the individuals and what they bring to the table. That does not just mean allowing everyone to participate and tolerating their opinions, but celebrating the diversity and regularly praising the team for it, such that they feel proud to be unique individuals and part of such a powerful team. Creating a team that wants to work together is not a difficult undertaking, as people innately want to belong. Having well-understood goals and vision for the team is then a prerequisite.

If you think well of your team, your team will thrive, but if you think or speak poorly of your team or even a few team members, as a team they will suffer and do badly. You cannot do anything about it except think well of everyone. You might now think of low performers, or people you inherited as a manager whom you would not have hired. You can address the situation either by finding something better suited for these people, or working to include the people such that they become contributing members of your team.

If you want to change your team culture to be more inclusive, in the beginning, you may need to *invite people to participate*, be it minorities or people who traditionally have been quieter. You need to make a conscious effort to ask people for their opinions and invite them to share their expertise. They may be so used to not being asked that they are overwhelmed at first. Or they may have had bad experiences in the past with speaking up and getting rejected. They may even be used to not having an opinion at all, because they were not asked or encouraged to think independently in the past. Anyhow, you first need to make them feel confident to speak up. Be careful not to put them on the spot and force them to say something. You need some patience up front. However, once people become comfortable speaking their minds, you will be rewarded with diverse insights and honest opinions and concerns. Overall, this will allow you to make better decisions.

It is important to understand that inclusion must come from the leader to be fully effective. First, the leader must understand what type of biases there could be in the team, be it personal or organizational, and then they need to create an environment of psychological safety for people to dare to speak up.

Sometimes it takes more than one person of a minority in a team to make these team members feel confident participating.

A PREREQUISITE FOR DIVERSITY

A colleague and board member of a large financial institution recently told me that he was part of a selection committee for new top managers. An executive position was offered to a very suitable woman, but she declined the offer because she feared she would not get enough support in the all-male team.

As the company was keen to raise diversity in their top management, in the next round, two positions were offered to two women. After brief consideration, both were happy to accept the offer since they could support each other. Everyone later agreed that these experienced women were real assets to have on the top management team.

Another way to be inclusive is to invite employees to *personally present the work they have done*, instead of presenting it yourself as the supervising manager. I have experienced that most managers are not willing to relinquish control of a presentation, because they do not trust the employees to be capable of adequately addressing the audience, who oftentimes consists of managers one or two levels above their own level. However, inclusion is also about enhancing the visibility of one's team members.

Any type of good *collaborative work* helps bring inclusion. This requires that you as the leader know the strengths of each individual team member and how to use them such that they complement each other. Collaboration requires that everyone's perspective is heard and that diverse ideas are welcomed, otherwise you will not get the range of views and opinions that is the benefit of diversity.

On the whole, we need to keep in mind that the effort toward equality is not a fight between men and women or minorities and majorities, but a reorientation away from outdated conditions towards more wholeness and more consciousness. Greater diversity, inclusion, and equality will lead to better collaboration, more sustainable decisions, higher-performing teams, better financial performance, and happier employees.

Summary

- To create an environment where employees bring their best to work, leaders need to make employees feel included and respected.

- With a diverse workforce and an inclusive environment, a company is able to create more innovative solutions and products that better serve its clients, employees, and other stakeholders. On the contrary, if a business is operated by a homogeneous group of people, there will be groupthink, which can be ineffective, as people will mostly confirm the leader's singular view.

- Humans do not tend to be naturally inclusive. Humans are prejudiced against people who are different or think differently. Prejudices can be open, meaning they are known to the person having them, or hidden, meaning that people are unaware of their own prejudices. This is also called unconscious bias.

- To achieve an inclusive workplace, one can either try to teach people to act inclusively, or companies can use behavioral design to build structures that force inclusive thinking. The latter tends to be less expensive and more effective.

- Some measures to increase diversity include the introduction of symmetric quotas, rethinking promotion and leadership criteria, taking care to use inclusive language, anonymization of application documents, and showing minority role models or examples of equality at work and in society.

- Diverse teams need to be managed inclusively. Otherwise, clashes between people of different cultures and ways of thinking can have a negative effect on productivity. Leading inclusively means valuing the contributions of all individuals and inviting them to openly share their views.

Exercises

1. Look back on our networking efforts and review who you have lunch with or otherwise spend time with who is below your level in the company hierarchy. Especially among people on your own team, consider how you can divide your time more fairly. It may not be the most natural way to network or spend your lunch time with certain

individuals, and it may even feel a little uncomfortable at first. After all, affinity bias makes you want to be around people who are similar to you. But planning to spend equal time with everyone on your team is a more diverse, inclusive, and fair way of networking. You will find over time that you are rewarded with other perspectives and new insight.

2. Reflect on the level of inclusiveness you have within your team. Are there areas where you could be more inclusive? Observe yourself during discussion meetings to see if all opinions are on the table. If not, brainstorm a few ways to encourage everyone to voice their viewpoints. More than likely, it will take some time before those who are used to keeping their opinions to themselves will be willing to share them openly.

3. Actively create opportunities for employees to demonstrate their skills. You could invite them to larger meetings to talk about their work rather than presenting it yourself, or you could let people present their own work in team meetings. This will expose the meeting attendees to new learning and new voices, as well as give the presenter a sense of inclusion and achievement.

4. Next time you hire a person, try to take the most unbiased approach, starting with writing the job application in a gender-neutral way, to selecting people for interviews using a partial-blind process with anonymized applications, to getting feedback from a diverse set of colleagues about each candidate. Reflect on whether the person finally hired would have been your first choice if you had followed your old process. You may find yourself pleasantly surprised.

Support your employees

Before you are a leader, success is all about growing yourself. When you become a leader, success is all about growing others.

—Jack Welch

As a leader, you have incredible power to help your employees flourish or to obstruct their growth. If you keep your employees small by just requesting that they do their work without looking left and right, you will not get much other than their daily work. If you encourage your employees to do excellent work and let them grow through exploration, you will get incredible work products from them which ultimately will make you and your team successful. It is a matter of choice how far you want to assert your influence; however, you need to realize that you are probably more influential than you think.

Bringing out the best in people requires deeply understanding what they need and what they are striving for. We have seen that life is about expanding happiness. It is about progress, having achievements, and feeling joy. In order to get a sense of achievement, people need to utilize their best skills, otherwise they do not feel fulfilled. Therefore, people need to be able to develop and expand their skills, such that they can grow and achieve even more. In fact, the opportunity to learn and grow is for many people more important than working solely to earn more money. Therefore, it is important for people to deeply *recognize their own abilities*, to *know what they really like to do* and *what they stand for* and *who they ultimately are*. In my experience, people do not normally know all this, or at least not with enough clarity. They might have an idea of what they are good at and what they like to do, but they would benefit greatly if they knew more about themselves. They would drift through life less and be able to move much more purposefully along their path towards realizing their full potential.

Besides achieving something for themselves, people need to feel recognition for their achievements. People also want to belong and be part of something greater than themselves.

As a leader, you have the great chance and honor to be part of your employees' journeys, to guide them, to affirm them, to recognize their achievements, to teach them, to help them grow, to lead them towards their best selves, to make them feel a sense of belonging. The more you invest in this kind of work, the more your employees will flourish, the more they will bring their best selves to work, the more they will achieve, and the more successful *you* will be. Additionally, they will be loyal to you and the company.

Develop your employees

Earlier, we talked about the importance of development for an individual. As a leader, especially for your direct reports, you will have a good sense of what they are really good at and also where they have room for improvement. Knowing what they strive for helps you to target your feedback and make suggestions about what they could develop. Encouraging people and developing talent are among a leader's main duties.

Take the time to find out what your direct reports want and what their motivation is. This can be in formal development sessions that are part of many organizations' regular procedures or ad hoc when the topic comes up. You can often also recognize a person's potential through observation and contemplation.

You would think that people generally would know what they want, what work they love to do, and what they are good at. But in my experience, many people often do not really know because they have not thought about it. Sometimes people might emulate someone they are genuinely not, or they follow popular trends to decide what they can and want to do. As their manager, you can figure this out with them. In my experience, once employees realized what they liked to do, they were much more motivated and became really good at their work. They did not necessarily need to change much, if anything, about what they did or how they did it, but just realizing what they are good at made them feel more inspired.

REALIZING WHAT YOU LIKE

I once had a mentee who was unhappy with his current work because he wanted a management position with personnel responsibility. However, the position he wanted was not available at that moment. We then analyzed what work he would do in the position he wanted and found that he already had the opportunity to do much of it in his current position, such as taking on a leadership perspective; he just was not aware of it. When he realized this, he was able to focus on being a leader in his current position. He was then motivated to do the rest of his work (which was necessary but not as exciting for him) in a short, focused period of time, leaving him more time for the leadership part of his current job. After he figured this out, he was much happier and more balanced.

Knowing what they love to do and what they want gives people direction and, along the way, helps them achieve things that will make them happy. In general, employees are not enough aware of what they love about their work. Becoming aware is the first step, and then they can organize their work around it. Things they love less, they can do quickly; things they love more, they can celebrate and enjoy. As an effect, they will become even better at the things they love.

Passion and talent are different for every person and can only be dealt with on an individual basis. The good thing about knowing this as a manager, however, is that you can distribute work in a more targeted way, such that you can better promote and support people, while also getting the best out of them.

Now, when you look at your entire team, people development can also mean offering your employees training in different areas to broaden their horizons, making them industry insiders and experts, or improving their soft skills. But people development is also giving feedback and making employees aware of their blind spots.

Giving genuine feedback

A part of the development of your employees is giving candid and helpful feedback. As a leader, it is your duty to give honest feedback. I have seen so many managers choose to be dishonest rather than explain themselves. They would rather avoid getting into an uncomfortable conversation than address unhelpful behaviors of their employees in order to help them improve.

SHINE LIGHT ON BLIND SPOTS

There were times in my management career when I could have been more candid, and looking at some cases in hindsight, I regret not having pushed people more to see their blind spots. Once, after I filled a position, I gave the rejected applicant reasons why he was not hired. I opted for reasons that were easy for him to understand, but those were probably not the main reasons why he had not gotten the job. Today, I regret not having told him that the real reason was lack of professionalism. However, I knew at the time that it would have taken a very difficult and lengthy talk to explain this to the applicant in detail. Yet that talk could have been to his advantage, because I suspect he had never heard this kind of feedback before. However, this talk never happened because my time was very limited back then, and my priority was coaching my own team.

Giving helpful feedback takes time, patience, diplomacy, and genuineness. Only then will it come across as effective and constructive feedback rather than criticism. It is not always easy, as pointing out someone's weak points can be uncomfortable and straining. However, if you have a trustful relationship with your employees and if they see that you really care about them, it will make it easier for them to understand. Additionally, asking them for feedback and making the feedback reciprocal helps too.

Even more important than giving candid feedback is giving *positive feedback*, or feedback on what is going well. Positive feedback is about reinforcing people's strengths, rather than trying to eliminate their weaknesses. It is about praising people, making them understand their skills and value. It will pull more energy towards the positive, creating more positive. Positivity will make people flourish. Just remember, where you put your thoughts, your energy will flow.

And the positivity will trickle down. Having good feedback sessions with your direct reports will raise the quality of the feedback sessions they have with *their* direct reports, and the entire team will be pushed forward. You will also get a better feel for how people think and what matters to them.

Showing appreciation

According to a Gallup study, employees who do not feel adequately recognized are twice as likely as those who do feel adequately recognized to say they will quit in the next year (Gallup 2017).

Whereas most people join companies for compensation, growth opportunities, or because they like the company's strategy or mission, many of these once optimistic people then leave due to a strained relationship with their managers. Not receiving appreciation prevents an employee from having a true sense of accomplishment or even a sense of belonging, both of which we have already seen are important to human beings. Therefore, people leave to search for happiness elsewhere. As a leader, this study should make you think about how to show appreciation to your teams.

There are so many things you can do to show your appreciation, and in my experience, it does not need to be anything extraordinary. It is more the daily appreciation you can show by seeing your employees, recognizing their work, valuing their efforts and achievements, and noting it by giving them a compliment or expressing gratitude in a simple note or "thank you." This can be in one-on-one conversations, but is often even more impactful if you do it in front of others, be it the team or other stakeholders. Also, recognizing someone at the beginning or the end of a meeting for having done something particularly well or contributing in a big way can have a huge impact. You can also praise your team to your own manager, who might mention your team in an even bigger meeting. Of course, this requires some thought on your part as to how to talk about your team's work and achievements in a way that interests and helps others see their importance. But the effort is worth it.

Some people think that if you praise your employees, they will become lazy because they will think they did enough or even too much, and thus decide that doing a little less would be sufficient too. In my experience, the opposite is the case. By sincerely praising people, you give them positive reinforcement to deliver even more next time. Human beings need recognition and appreciation like they need nourishment.

THE RIGHT FEEDBACK

I once had a manager who was particularly good at giving me feedback. It was mostly positive feedback, and he always expressed his gratitude for my work. If there was something he wanted improved, he made suggestions on how to do it differently. The prevailing impression during and after such a meeting was positive, and I usually ran back to my office to do whatever we had discussed and stayed late until it was finished.

Some years later, I had a manager who was proud of his ability to give candid feedback. If he was not happy with a work product, he told you so directly. After meetings with him, his negative tone always made me think that he should just do the work himself and I would leave the office at least an hour earlier than usual that day.

Superior people praise; inferior people criticize and diminish others. Nothing raises self-confidence in a person more than praise, and nothing diminishes self-confidence more than criticism or making people feel they do not belong. Hence, if you want to have self-confident employees who flourish, praise them often. If you yourself do not get praise as much as you like, then praise yourself as often as you can. This also helps your self-confidence. By no means should you give praise only for big achievements, like finishing a project or reaching an important milestone, but also recognize smaller achievements on the way to achieving bigger goals.

Some people are not used to giving compliments, and often the same people are not used to receiving compliments or feel awkward receiving them. To overcome the first, it is important to practice giving compliments often, at least daily. Start small with feeling and expressing gratitude. Then, you can go further with making targeted compliments, for instance about an employee's work product or commendable effort. To overcome the second, you must learn to accept compliments and not diminish whatever they were recognizing. Just say "thank you" without making further comments, whether you think the compliment is justified or not, or be truly honest and say for instance that you also think you made a big effort to complete your good work. In any case, be prepared to receive more compliments when you start giving compliments to others, as this will naturally happen according to the universal law of giving and receiving. It will have the nice effect of increasing your self-confidence in addition.

There are obviously other measures to show appreciation, like giving an employee a day off, an extra bonus, a promotion, or a salary raise, but typically, the happiness these events bring does not last for long. Also, some company cultures like to have "employee of the month" awards or something similar. However, this can quickly breed jealousy among the employees and is, in my view, not helpful in a global context, neither in the short nor in the long run.

Showing appreciation also means showing interest in someone's life. The more you know about their lives outside of work, the more you can show your appreciation by being flexible on what is going on with your employees, and they will thank you in kind with flexibility and commitment. The more compassion you show and the more you care for your employees, the more they will also develop a sense of belonging, which will lead to loyalty on their part.

You might have employees for whom you have difficulties finding positive contributions and you rather find points to criticize. There is nothing wrong with giving objective targeted feedback on how to make things better without being overly critical. However, at the same time, try hard to find things you can positively point out or praise, because praise, thanks, encouragement, and coaching will help much more to get the best out of your employees. With praise, they will go beyond the call of duty, beyond what you expected, and maybe even beyond what they imagined for themselves.

Keeping employees engaged pays off. A Gallup study showed that business units with engaged workers result in 23 percent greater profitability compared to business units with unhappy workers, because they are more process driven, more productive, and more attentive to customers (Gallup 2022). In addition, every kindness you give to your employees will come back to you.

Emphasize diverse hiring

When hiring for the most important roles on your team, namely those that report directly to you, it is worth walking the extra mile to find the right person.

I always keep in mind what the investor Warren Buffett said: "One of the best things you can do in life is to surround yourself with people who are better than you are." They do not necessarily need to know more than you in any field, but they should complement you and push you to be better too. The outcome is that you will hire a diverse and intelligent workforce made up of individuals who have integrity. The people you surround yourself with will also influence you. The more time you spend with them, the more they will influence you. If you give them what they need—good work, opportunities to grow, general attention, and appreciation—you will get the best out of them and out of *yourself* too.

However, if you hire employees who are technically brilliant but have a difficult mentality, whether they are cynical, inflexible, jealous, or distrustful, you will have a lot of work bringing them to the point where they can focus on the matter and not on others. In addition, they will negatively influence you and the rest of the team. You would need a lot of energy not to be influenced. And although it is not impossible for these people to adapt, it would take a lot more work on your part to integrate them into a net-positive culture. In such cases, it helps to see their potential and their very own good essence. It may be easier to prolong the search until you find someone with brilliant skills, both technically and personally.

Likewise, if you inherit a team and find their mindset to be overall negative and not inclusive, do not go about trying to replace the entire team just yet. You can teach them the principles of this book, starting with positive thinking and clearing out unhelpful beliefs and so on, to bring them towards corporate life mastery.

Foster inclusion

We saw before that people long to belong, not only outside of work but also at work, where we spend the majority of our days. We spend too much time at work to only get a sense of belonging in our spare time. As a leader, you have the great opportunity to create an atmosphere where people can feel that sense of belonging and being part of a community. It all starts with inclusion and creating a space where employees feel *psychologically safe* to speak up. The more people feel their opinion matters and the more they feel heard, the more they will open up and share their views. As a result, you will have a more diverse decision basis and you will be rewarded with more innovation.

Sometimes, making sure that everyone gets time to speak in discussions or team meetings requires a certain coordination effort. You have surely experienced meetings where some people talk all the time, while others do not speak at all. Both extremes are not nice. It is not that the ones talking all the time have that much to say; they often repeat what they have already said, when it only needs to be said once. Those who are quiet probably have an opinion, too, and might contribute to more diverse fact-finding and better decision-making. Hence, you are challenged as a leader to make sure *all* ideas are heard. This involves teaching the whole team attentive listening skills as a prerequisite, and practicing them yourself.

Also, when new employees join the team, be as inclusive as possible. Make sure they can connect to other people on your team as well as outside of your team.

Not feeling a sense of belonging on a team isolates people and makes them lonely. They will certainly not be as energized and motivated to bring their best to work under these circumstances.

To foster your employees to speak up, you can give them a platform to make themselves visible, whether it is by letting them present in a team meeting or organizing discussion rounds. With time, they will become more used to speaking confidently. Most important is to create a space of trust and respect. The collaborative and inclusive environment will intellectually stimulate your employees, as they will be forced to think for themselves and have an opinion. It will make them learn faster so that they feel confident sharing their views. Hence, the more opportunities they get to speak their minds and be visible, the faster they will learn and evolve.

Do not allow employees to overwork themselves

Corporations today care more about their employees' well-being than in the past, as it has been found that there is a direct link between employee well-being and company performance. Mentally and physically healthy employees are more engaged, less stressed, and take fewer sick days, and therefore are more productive.

Well-being initiatives may entail sessions on mental health awareness, well-being workshops, the introduction of more flexible working styles, offerings of yoga classes, and more. However, as much as a company-wide employee wellness program makes sense, it is the manager who can contribute most to employee well-being.

If you truly care about your employees, do not let them overwork. Do not give them more and more work until they collapse. Instead, when you give them extra work, take something else off their agenda. Not letting your employees overwork can be tricky if you overwork yourself, as you will probably not notice when others are overwhelmed. Keep in mind that constant overwork is unsustainable for your health. There is nothing wrong with having crunch times where people have to put in more work, be it to close the books or finish a project. A particularly intense period sometimes even energizes people and gives them excitement and a great sense of achievement when they have met a deadline. However, they need to be able to balance out that stress soon, whether by taking some days off or enjoying a few shorter workdays. Otherwise, you will exhaust, frustrate, and burn people out.

Make sure you lead by example to demonstrate what is a reasonable work-life balance. Praise those who know how to prioritize work and life so that the others learn from them. Overworked employees who work long hours do not deliver more quality and value than engaged employees who work normal hours.

Also, you need to pay special attention to people with low self-esteem.

Unfortunately, they often tend to overwork, as they will not fight back when they are given too much work. They will just silently take on what you give them until it becomes obvious that they cannot cope with everything that is on their plate. Also, it is particularly important for them to receive appreciation for their work, and giving praise regularly can gradually raise their self-esteem.

But it is not only those with low self-esteem who need appreciation—*everyone needs appreciation.* If you as a leader create an environment where employees feel appreciated for the work they do, they will not need to work more and more and more trying to earn appreciation. After too many hours of work, quality decreases anyway. If you find people are consistently working overtime, you may also want to examine the immediate causes. Probably they are distracted by too many meetings, and, therefore, they do not have the time they need to do their actual work. Or they have too many emails to follow and respond to. Or your company has too many workflow tools that need to be completed, taking priority over the work itself. In addition to relieving some of the external load, you can teach employees how to manage their energy. However, the most promising approach is to get to the root of employee wellness and create a culture of appreciation and gratitude. With that, not only you as a leader will give appreciation and drive the team forward with positivity, but your team also will get in the habit of showing appreciation toward each other.

Just remember, a fulfilled life is about expanding happiness. Expansion comes with growing, growing comes from achieving, and that great feeling of achievement comes from acknowledgment and appreciation from others and also yourself for the work you do. Therefore, appreciation is the key to expanding happiness.

Summary

- Leaders are highly influential in pushing employees to deliver excellent work and letting them grow. If they understand that people ultimately strive for expanding happiness, meaning progress and achievement, they are able to bring the very best out of people.

- Recognizing your employees' abilities, knowing what they really like to do and what they stand for and who they ultimately are, is important for being able to help them flourish and realize their full potential.

- Giving honest feedback to your employees about their blind spots is as important as giving them positive feedback about what works well. This is about reinforcing people's strengths, rather than trying to eliminate weaknesses.

- Giving appreciation to employees raises their sense of accomplishment. This can be a promotion or a salary raise, but more frequent appreciation by recognizing their work and efforts and by saying "thank you" can be even more effective.

- Praising people raises their self-confidence; making them feel they do not belong diminishes their self-confidence. Hence, if you want to have self-confident employees who flourish, you should praise them often.

- To make people feel that they belong, a leader needs to create an atmosphere of inclusion where employees feel psychologically safe to speak up and share their views. If they feel they can genuinely contribute, employees will be motivated to bring their best to work.

Exercises

1. Think about how much you know about your direct reports. Do you really know their strengths? Do you know what they want? Do you know what they stand for? Do you think they themselves know it? If not, make a plan to learn more about them and together, translate that conversation into a personal development plan.

2. How often do you show your appreciation to your employees? If you feel you could recognize their work, efforts, and achievements more often, make a plan on how to do that. Whom will you recognize and

when? What will you say or what gesture of appreciation will you give? Do this for several weeks and reflect afterwards about what has changed. Doing this exercise consistently for long enough will create a culture of gratitude within your team.

3. Reflect about the inclusion and listening skills of your team. If you find these skills to be lacking in any way, arrange a workshop to teach them as much as you think is necessary to create an atmosphere of inclusion and belonging.

Support your team

Be the most ethical, the most responsible, the most authentic you can be with every breath you take, because you are cutting a path into tomorrow that others will follow.
—Ken Wilber

As a leader, you have several ways to positively influence your team and get your employees to work together so that everyone brings their best to work. In fact, you can significantly support your team to reach corporate life mastery together. Whether you teach them about finding purpose, developing meaningful goals, how to collaborate, or you lay the groundwork so they can easily expand their knowledge and networks, as a leader you have great potential to influence your team.

By explaining these concepts to them well, you can quickly get them to the point where they enjoy their work, find meaning in what they do, become more self-confident, and contribute to their fullest capabilities. You have the power to lead your team to do their work with ease and joy. With that, you inevitably will become a role model.

Use team meetings wisely

One way to directly impact your team is through team meetings. Depending on the size of the team, these meetings work differently, but typically they are used to ensure people are aligned, collectively discuss and understand current issues, and give the opportunity to ask questions. Additionally, you can use team meetings to celebrate successes, show appreciation, and build relationships.

Depending on the size of the team, you can have people share something personal, which greatly increases their sense of belonging.

HONORING YOUR PEOPLE

I used to start our monthly global team meetings, where people would call in from all over the world, with a short presentation by a person or sub-team on a particular topic. For a while, we had a theme of "How We Celebrate," where employees from a particular part of the world shared a local festive custom. This ranged from a first birthday celebration in South Korea, to the Bavarian Oktoberfest, to the carnival in Rio, to a wedding in Swaziland, to the green Chicago River on St. Patrick's Day. These presentations of course used up precious time, and there was always the risk that people's explanations would run too long, but there was a special atmosphere of fun, individuality, contribution, and belonging that was more than rewarding.

I highly recommend starting every meeting with a positive message, such as by sharing something personal or presenting something positive about the team or the company. This can be very short, but the result—that the actual meeting will start on a positive note—is huge. Never start a meeting with something negative. You will have much more difficulty bringing the course back to engage people positively. Of course, as an exception, I would refrain from doing this if you are communicating very bad news like layoffs and the like.

Another way to directly impact your team is through organizing common learning sessions. These can be about technical or soft skills you want them to acquire, current business trends, or other units of the corporation. These sessions will make sure everyone is up to date and knowledgeable about the business. These types of meetings additionally give a sense of belonging to the participants if they learn together about topics of concern.

However, you might find there are already too many meetings and that it does not make sense to add another one to your team's calendar. In any case, you must know yourself how best to influence your employees, how to inform them, and how to make them feel like they belong. Which planning techniques and strategies you use to accomplish this is up to you. For me, having a regular meeting was the simplest measure to achieve this. Just keep in mind that life is about expansion—expanding your knowledge, your circle of influence, your network, your impact. When you give this to your employees, they will feel fulfilled and will bring their best to work.

Talk purpose

We saw earlier how finding purpose in the work we do is helpful in many ways. It makes us feel that what we do matters, that we belong to something bigger than ourselves, and it makes us engage with our work more, as doing so gives us meaning. There is more trust and loyalty among the employees as well as with customers. Studies have even shown that companies whose employees, in particular middle management and professional staff, have strong beliefs in the meaning of their work experience better performance (Gartenberg et al. 2016). These companies with a defined corporate purpose beyond just making money have more long-term success and individuals working there stay longer, feel more contentment, and live overall healthier lives.

If you are interested in how to find the purpose of your team, you can find guidance in *Find Your Why* by Simon Sinek et al. (2017). In this book, the authors describe how you can structure workshops with your team to come up with a "why statement." Involving team members in coming up with a team's purpose makes it stronger, as it guarantees that the statement resonates with them. If your company has an overall purpose already defined, you should try to tie it to your team's purpose.

Once you have defined the purpose of the team, every employee can relate it to their own personal purpose. It allows people to deeply connect with their work and the business on a personal level. Your personal purpose is why you do what you do. Your purpose inspires and motivates you. You can determine your purpose by asking yourself what you love to do, what you are good at, and most importantly, what you want to do for others.

Understanding how one's personal purpose connects to the purpose of one's team or company will greatly motivate your employees. They will not only love to come to work, but they will also bring their best to work and leave work each day contented about what they have achieved. When you start with purpose, then performance and financial results will inevitably follow. This is because focusing on purpose allows people to fully concentrate on the work without having to think that they potentially would like to do something different that gives them more meaning. Most people will be convinced that they are good at the place they are at, or if not, they will know what to look for that will give them more meaning. In any case, they will understand the deeper sense of what they are currently doing and why.

The benefit of putting purpose *before* financial results is that it will make people work more ethically and lead them to follow a longer-term strategy. Research shows that companies with a strong purpose also perform better economically, and the employee retention rate is high. Hence, make sure you talk about your team's purpose often and show how the day-to-day activities relate to it.

Work on meaningful goals

Your job as a leader is to hire and engage the best talent. It is also your responsibility to come up with meaningful goals for your whole team. The best approach by far is to let the team come up with its own set of goals, giving as input your team's purpose and overall departmental and company goals. You know it from yourself: The more you are involved in defining your own business goals, the more you will stand behind them. Not only is there more motivation to achieve them, but the chances are higher that the individuals, and therefore the whole team and you, will achieve the goals.

If goals are imposed on employees with little room for self-determination on the overarching targets, employees may feel insignificant, bossed around, or powerless.

In any case, if you want to retain your high-performers, it is best to let them participate in the design and future of your team. Also make sure you show that you have high expectations of them and work with them to write ambitious, challenging individual goals so that they feel a true sense of achievement. If you set goals that are too easy to achieve, they will not be able to fully enjoy their achievements. They will not experience flow. They may feel underutilized, and they may start looking around for something bigger to achieve.

Whether an employee is a high-performer or not, they will be greatly inspired to achieve their goals if you have helped them formulate demanding individual goals and, in addition, created a caring environment with supportive and helpful team members. Of course, proving this requires a way to transparently track progress on these goals.

Treat your employees as your most precious asset by giving them encouragement, support, and acknowledgement and helping them to grow. If you work with them on meaningful goals and then let them make their own decisions and take ownership of their work, they will get a sense of achievement, they will need less external motivation, they will flourish and bring their best to work. They will thank you with their loyalty and support. As a result, you will not only have great success, but also find satisfaction and joy in being a leader. Your team collectively with you will achieve corporate life mastery.

Make them work together

An important task for you as a leader is making people feel they belong, bringing them to work well together. The more your employees feel they belong to your team and the company, the more they will be motivated and feel safe to state their opinions, the more they will give to the team, and the more they will be able to receive from the team. Hence, if people feel they belong, collaboration is better and productivity is higher, and this results in higher employee retention.

Belonging is even more important if you head a virtual team, meaning team members are not working in the same physical location. People working remotely can more easily feel isolated, which can result in lower commitment and engagement, especially for tasks that need collaboration. You may notice that these employees have lower motivation and take more sick days, and you may have more turnover in your team overall. As a leader, you must make sure no one feels excluded. You can take the following actions to create a sense of belonging among your employees:

- Accept your employees as they are. Do not favor any one over the other.

- Keep in personal contact with your employees, especially if you head a virtual team.

- Support your employees in their daily work and career development.

- Set up situations that make people work together. You can build cross-team groups to solve problems or work on initiatives. In case some employees have work that does not require them to have much interaction with others, or they always interact only with the same few people, try to create little tasks that require these employees to collaborate with others. This could be organizing something, like an initiative around workplace culture, a learning session, or even a party or get-together.

- Introduce opportunities for mentoring, where more experienced team members mentor less experienced ones or newcomers.

- As a leader, you can even make inclusion and belonging a topic of work in itself for you and your team. Try to work together to find ways to make your team members feel included and enhance belonging.

However, feelings of isolation and not belonging can be subtle, and people may not be fully aware of who on the team excludes others or is the one being excluded. In such cases, awareness to the situation is the first step to enhancing everyone's belonging.

Sometimes, employees put too much weight on belonging to a team and a company and make their happiness dependent on how things go at work. In general, you should not make your happiness too much dependent on others, and certainly not on a company. There will be situations in the work environment that are beyond your control, for instance, if you are no longer supported by a new manager, or you are laid off due to external circumstances. In such cases, it can be devastating when people are suddenly left out of the job where they found their sole happiness and sense of belonging. It is also up to you as a leader to recognize such cases and ensure that these people open up to broader perspectives.

Task immersion

One of my initiatives as a manager was to introduce a learning program, first with my team and then for a large department, which combined learning from others, fostered joint work, and created networking opportunities for those involved.

The idea was that employees came up with their own tasks that other people could be interested to learn something about. Employees from across the department could then enroll to learn any task they wanted out of the ones their colleagues were offering to teach. The two parties would agree on a schedule together, and then the work would start. First, people were introduced to the task in a few hours by the knowledgeable employee. Later, they would take part in the task when it needed to be performed, and ideally, they had some work steps to do on their own to help complete that task. Afterwards, they had to give a brief presentation on the results of this task exchange, for instance to more senior management. After a short debrief, the learning session was completed. The timeline of a learning cycle typically ranged from a few hours to a few days, depending on the nature of the task.

This system of learning went beyond simple job shadowing, as it required the participants to do some work on their own. With that system, employees could immerse in a task and extend their knowledge. Given that they had to do some work on their own, it was almost inevitable that they learned something. Furthermore, they had the chance to get to know new people and extend their network. This learning model could also be used as a low-threshold way for people thinking about a next position to test out potential teams. Another nice side effect was that people got to share their work with others, which sometimes forced them to stretch their comfort zone, while making them feel important and giving them pride in their own work and building their self-confidence overall. It also created a sense of bonding and belonging. And participation was entirely voluntary, so it helped people be accountable for their own personal development.

The whole organization of the system was so spread out that it was a small investment for everyone but led to a large outcome for knowledge sharing and people development. Some overall coordination was necessary, but not a lot. It entailed mainly collecting a list of tasks people wanted to teach, soliciting applications from people who were interested in learning, and creating the annual report at the end of it all. Everything else was self-organized between the independent teachers and students. Once a year, the entire system was analyzed, to look at how many tasks were offered, how many people enrolled to learn a task, and how many actually performed what they set out to learn. In addition, the company collected feedback that showed that in the cases where a full cycle of task learning actually took place, people found it to be a great experience, not only because they learned something, but also from a personal perspective of growth and expanding one's network.

Summary

- Well-organized team meetings, where the team members can contribute not only professionally but also personally, where leaders take time to celebrate success and show appreciation, contribute to a good team spirit, and make team members feel they belong. Starting on a positive note lifts the entire meeting, whereas starting with a negative note will make it difficult to bring the meeting back to a normal level.

- As leaders, we can positively influence our teams by investing time into finding purpose for our team and for individual team members.

This makes team members feel that what they do matters and makes them more engaged, as their work now gives them meaning.

- Letting the team come up with its own set of goals—given the team's purpose, input from the leader, and overall departmental and company goals—leads to more motivation to achieve them.

- High-performers need to be held to high expectations and they need ambitious, challenging individual goals to feel a true sense of achievement. With goals that are too easy, they will not be able to fully enjoy their achievements and may feel underutilized, and they may look around for something bigger to achieve.

- Cross-team work raises employees' sense of belonging. If they feel they belong to the team or company, they are likely to be motivated, feel safe stating their opinions, and collaborate more effectively, which results in higher productivity and higher employee retention.

- Task immersion programs, where employees can learn from others about their tasks and even do hands-on work contributing to these tasks, are a good means to employee development. It extends the employees' networks, fosters collaboration, and can be used as a low-threshold way to test out potential teams for people thinking about internally moving to their next position.

Exercises

1. Think about your team meetings and how you could start them on a positive note. You might let people present something personal, for instance a favorite object, or a holiday story, or a favorite joke. You could also present something positive yourself at the beginning of the meeting, like a good collaboration you have observed or good results of a team, and so on.

   After two or three meetings where you pushed for a positive start, reflect on how the meetings went from there. Chances are high that they turned out to be friendly and, more importantly, constructive.

2. Do a self-assessment of how well your employees feel they belong to the team and the company. You will often find questions around this topic in annual anonymous employee surveys. Look for questions like those asking employees to rate how much they agree with statements like "I am proud of working at this company," "There is open and honest communication at this company," or "I feel valued by my team." You can take these questions for your survey, or craft something similar.

Then discuss your self-assessment with your leadership team. Do they feel the need to strengthen their and their employees' sense of belonging? To take your efforts a step further, organize an awareness session with your leadership team about how important it is for employees to feel a sense of belonging.

3. Make a conscious effort to accept your employees as they are and not favor any one over the other. Think about the members of your team and write down something positive for each person. This can be something you find appealing about their character or skills, or it can be something lighter like the style of clothing they wear. Just come up with something.

Next time before you talk to them, remind yourself of what you wrote down about them. You will have a better encounter, they will feel a little more accepted, and most likely they will accept you a little more too.

4. Consider whether a program like the task immersion program could benefit your team. If yes, set about organizing and implementing it. Talk to a few team members about it, and enlist the help of one who enjoys organizing to run it.

CONCLUSION

I am not what happened to me, I am what I decide to become.
—Carl Gustav Jung

You have read it several times in this book: Life is about expanding happiness. Everything in the universe is expanding, and the universe itself is expanding too. Whatever does not grow is slowly dying. The fact that we are expanding is confirmed by our sense of achievement and success. Achievement makes us feel happy and satisfied. However, what we perceive as achievement and success is very personal. For some, finishing a report at work leaves a great feeling of accomplishment, and they go home feeling totally content; for others, finishing the same report is a dull repetition, and they finish the workday only happy that it is over. If you are someone who struggles with work that has become meaningless and repetitive to you and you feel you are not expanding personally in whatever way, you need to think about what brings you joy and contentment at work. The first step is to look for ways you can further grow at your current workplace or in your current role. In many cases, I have seen this is very possible if someone can identify the parts of their work they enjoy and find meaningful. However, if you cannot grow anymore at your current workplace, then it is time to advance to your next position, and you need to take this next step with a clear understanding of where you want to grow and expand.

In order to understand where you need to grow and find purpose, it is best to look *inside*. No one else can advise you better than yourself. Of course, you can ask your manager, mentors, or colleagues for advice. They can help you by giving you outside perspective, but you should start and end by looking inside. This means knowing what you want, which essentially means knowing who you are, what you love, and what your specific strengths and values are. The journey towards knowing this will lead you to go deep and is ultimately highly rewarding. If you know your strengths, you can build on them. If you know what is meaningful to you, you can formulate goals. With that, you will have a North Star to guide your decisions. Whenever you are unsure about which way to go, you need to remind yourself of who you are. And when you find something that gives you a sense of joy, you can be sure that it is the right choice in that moment. Actions that go in the direction of expansion and joy will bring you happiness and fulfillment, and you will have a sense of purpose in your life. Living in alignment with your values and purpose will make everything in life flow much easier and will bring you great success.

If, on the other hand, you do not give any thought to who you are and remain unaware, you are not radiating your values. People will guess who you are, and they may interpret something in you that you may not agree with. To avoid this, you must know your values and radiate them. The more you know your strengths, the more you can leverage them and the more you can impact other people's lives. Hence, it is important to develop your expertise, to become good in something that you like doing. Being skilled in an area and becoming an expert in a field will give you great satisfaction and contentment. Next to being skilled in the field you enjoy, influencing others as well as communicating effectively will always help. Altogether, this will almost guarantee you a good career and job security. As we have seen, financial abundance will follow as an effect of your competency, value, and service to others.

Living your best work life and advancing does not mean you have to completely change what you have done so far just because doing something totally different might possibly bring you more joy. Instead, you need to find out how you can build upon what you have done so far. There will be things you love to do and other things you do not enjoy so much. Find out what you love to do and do more of it: expand it; learn more about it; make it a specialty that others seek you out for. For the rest that you do not love and actually want to do less of—but need to do—do it concentratedly and intensely and expeditiously so that it is quickly over. Apply the 20:80 rule, meaning with 20 percent of effort, you will get 80 percent done. In the corporate world, it is often better to produce results than to work on making something perfect or beautiful. Concentrating on the essence of a task is oftentimes sufficient. There will be instances, though, where you will need more than 80 percent; in those cases, use your good judgement.

The ability to control your thoughts is a very basic skill needed for mastering your corporate life. It does not only entail being aware of what you are thinking, but also being able to actively break negative thought patterns and positively influence what happens in your life by thinking supportive thoughts about whatever you want to do or achieve. Thinking highly of yourself is paramount. Be a good friend to yourself and stop negative self-talk and self-criticism. You can reflect on yourself, but without judging. Promote yourself and surround yourself with uplifting, optimistic people and you will become one of them too.

Your professional and personal success depend on how you think about things. As explained earlier, if you think your project is going to fail, chances are high that it will indeed end that way. On the other hand, if you think your project will be a big success, this will likely come to fruition. This is because your underlying beliefs will lead you to make different little decisions on your way. It is your inner attitude and positive thought management that will bring you success. Success actually comes from within. Your mindset is decisive of that. Therefore, be careful of what you think and the words you use.

In order to advance according to your wishes, you will need to understand what it takes to get promoted or selected for the position you want. In most corporations, one of the most important things is to be visible to the people who decide on promotions and hiring. Hence, working on your visibility by presenting your work, speaking up in meetings, and networking in style is paramount. Your most excellent work will not be of much worth to you if no one other than your manager or your peers know about it. In such case, if your manager does not promote you to his or her peers and upper-level managers, it could be because he or she wants to keep such an excellent employee for a while, chances are small that you will get promoted or that other opportunities will open up to you in the same corporation. Just recall, people with high social capital, meaning those who have a solid network, receive more help from others. In addition, people are promoted who are easy to work with, have good communication skills, are reliable, and have a professional, positive attitude.

In the end, living who you are, living your values, building on your strengths, and learning the things you would love to do will bring you great contentment and fulfillment. It will also make you more self-confident, which is a large part of an abundant and happy life.

If you are a leader, make sure you teach all of the above to your employees. Lay the groundwork for them to flourish, help them to develop, and want them to be themselves instead of wanting them to change to your wishes. Taking them as they are with their strengths and weaknesses will guide you on how to develop them. Keep in mind that life is about expansion and development. Hence, it is the opportunity to learn, growing their responsibilities, and contributing to others that motivates your employees more than just earning more money. Also remember that it is important to confirm your team's development by recognizing their achievements, individually and as a team. Do not hold back with expressing praise and gratitude for your employees' accomplishments. With positive feedback, they will bring their best to work and will not only make themselves successful, but also help you succeed as a leader.

This book may not seem to be about traditional business values such as results, profitability, and the creation of economic value. You may feel like you have missed them along the way in our discussion. In fact, the opposite is true. When leaders take good care of their employees, they will be more productive, more creative, and higher performing. They will flourish and bring their whole body, mind, and soul to work. They will not distractedly long to get off work or wait for the weekend to feel alive. Given the problems we face today as a society and as inhabitants of our planet, it has become increasingly important for companies to find solutions to pressing issues. To do this, we need a motivated workforce that is happy to give its best. For everyone to give their best, companies need inclusive cultures where people are understood and promoted as individuals, and where everyone is invited to contribute.

Kindness, compassion, appreciation, and praise, *not* demand, control, blame and shame, will be what drives us forward in the future.

This sort of inclusive future requires that everyone balances their feminine and masculine qualities without suppressing one or the other. There also needs to be a shift in thinking about why we move forward. Until now, many people believe that evolution occurs solely to avoid pain and deal with scarcity. However, evolution also happens because of curiosity and, above all, joy and excitement. People do not work only to avoid pain, nor do they succeed only by making sacrifices. They also work for joy, especially the joy of achievement. Always allow joy to enter your work life. By no means does a happy workforce mean a lazy and unproductive one. On the contrary, a happy workforce is a positive, engaged, and resilient workforce that strives and thrives and takes the organization to a new level.

Remember, there is no one absolute truth. Everyone has his or her view of the world. When you really internalize this, you will realize you do not have to spend your energy fighting about being right. In most cases, you can instead concentrate on problem-solving and moving forward. The same is true for this book: You do not have to judge what in it is right or wrong. Simply take what you find works for you. There is no single path to success. Rather, you should follow and implement what appeals to you. Use your energy for something that will bring you forward. In most cases, "being right" will not bring you forward. Insisting on it only steals your time, which you could use for better things. Also, it is much easier to criticize than to make an effort to change, which is why people complain so often. Instead, take accountability for your own life and see what you can do next.

Like everything in life, knowing about something in theory is usually not enough; doing it repeatedly in practice is the key to success. When you decide on moving forward, also do not wait for some permission or invitation from the outside to come into action. It is your responsibility to move forward. If you do not decide and instead just let things happen, chances are that you will be used to make someone else's dreams come true. Keep in mind that not deciding is also a decision, and comfortable inaction carries more risks to your happiness than you might initially think.

If you have decided to change and move forward, be aware that change starts in your mind. By changing your thoughts and talking positively to yourself about what you want to achieve, your conscious and subconscious mind will act on it accordingly and you will succeed easily.

Along the way, try to become aware of what has led to success, what you like to do, what brings you into the flow, where you feel sparks of joy. Knowing this will help you advance more quickly and make the way smoother. Knowing what you want and who you are also raises your self-esteem, as do achievement and feeling proud of yourself. I cannot stress enough how important it is to always think highly of yourself. Do not diminish yourself or allow negative self-talk to chatter on in your head. Always remember that you are on *your* side. Backing yourself makes you more confident, and with that you will value yourself more, which in turn will cause others to value you more and could even result in a higher remuneration of your work.

We have seen earlier how important a good network is. It is not the sheer size of the network, but more the quality of people. Those who will help you and those who you can help. Always keep in mind that contributing and helping others will make you advance faster too.

I hope this book brought more clarity to your work life, to your thoughts and beliefs, your values, and how to fulfill your potential. Summarizing everything, my top tips for success are as follows:

- Be conscious of your thoughts, and free yourself from limiting beliefs and false judgements.

- Know what you want, find meaning in what you do, and dream big.

- Know who you are, be passionate about your values, and radiate them.

- Write down your goals and make a feasible, prioritized action plan that you review regularly.

- Do not wait for inspiration or invitation from others before you act. Take initiative to pursue your goals and to reach achievements and results.

- Make a commitment to grow daily, and to go beyond theory and apply what you learn.

- Always seek the good in people. Help them develop and allow them to flourish by adopting an inclusive mindset.

- Be as effective as possible by being organized and by managing your energy so that you have enough for the important things in life, as well as to advance your action plan.

- Be fully present, connect with people, and make your voice heard.

- Invest in good relationships and always consider how you can help others.

- Be your own best friend and supporter. Think kindly and highly of yourself. Value and praise yourself often.

- Follow joy and excitement!

The way to mastering corporate life is a journey. It is like learning to ride a wave. You fall into the water over and over in the beginning, and then occasionally you manage to stand up on the board for a certain time. With more practice, but also good coaches and knowledge about how to best do it, keeping your balance becomes easier and easier. Staying motivated and keeping at it eventually allows you to master the waves with grace, ease, and joy. Achieving corporate life mastery is exactly the same. In the beginning, you will fail and learn from your mistakes. Later, by applying what you have learned in this book and elsewhere, you will become increasingly self-aware and self-assured. You will succeed in the things you set your mind to. You will be able to have an extraordinary, unique career that is fully in line with what you want and who you are. With corporate life mastery, you will achieve success with grace, ease, and joy. Feeling the resulting happiness and expanding it will be life changing, I assure you.

I wish you well on your journey towards mastering your corporate life and I would be delighted to hear from you about your experiences with my book. You can contact me at www.corporatelifemastery.com. Thank you very much!

YOUR NEXT STEPS

The amount of good luck coming your way
depends on your willingness to act.
—Barbara Sher

If you would like to deepen the impact of this book on your life, you can join a transformation program and attend a course offered at www.corporatelifemastery.com/signature. There, you will have the opportunity to work in small groups spread over several weeks, ensuring optimal learning and deep transformation.

You can sign up at www.corporatelifemastery.com/contact.

YOUR NEXT STEPS

LITERATURE

Achor, Shawn. 2010. *The Happiness Advantage*. Virgin Digital.

Allen, David. 2001. *Getting Things Done: The Art of Stress-Free Productivity*. Penguin Group.

Bauhofer, Ulrich. 2020. *Mehr Energie: Wie wir in Balance leben* (More energy: How we live in balance). NordSüd.

Ben-Shahar, Tal. 2007. *Happier: Learn the Secrets of Daily Joy and Lasting Fulfillment*. McGraw-Hill.

Bohnet, Iris. 2016. *What Works: Gender Equality by Design*. The Belknap Press of Harvard University Press.

Burkus, David. 2018. *Friend of a Friend . . . Understanding the Hidden Networks That Can Transform Your Life and Your Career*. Houghton Mifflin Harcourt Publishing Company.

Burnett, Bill, and Dave Evans. 2016. *Designing Your Life: How to Build a Well-Lived, Joyful Life*. Alfred A. Knopf Publisher.

Burt, Ronald S. 1995. *Structural Holes—The Social Structure of Competition*. Harvard University Press.

Chopra, Deepak. 1994. *The Seven Spiritual Laws of Success*. Amber-Allen Publishing and New World Library.

Covey, Stephen R. 1989. *The 7 Habits of Highly Effective People*. Simon & Schuster.

Csikszentmihalyi, Mihaly. 1990. *Flow: The Psychology of Optimal Experience*. Harper Perennial.

Cuddy, Amy. 2015. *Presence—Bringing your Boldest Self to Your Biggest Challenges*. Orion.

Dunbar, Robin. 2016. *Human Evolution: Our Brains and Behavior*. Oxford University Press.

Dweck, Carol S. 2006. *Mindset—Changing the Way You Think to Fulfill Your Potential*. Random House.

Eurich, Tasha. 2017. *Insight: How Small Gains in Self-Awareness Can Help You Win Big at Work and at Life*. Currency/Penguin.

Eyal, Nir, and Julie Li. 2019. *Indistractable: How to Control Your Attention and Choose Your Life*. Bloomsbury Publishing.

Gallup State of the American Workplace 2017 Report. www.gallup.com.

Gallup State of the Global Workplace 2022 Report—The Voice of the World's Employees. www.gallup.com.

García, Héctor, and Francesc Miralles. 2016. *Ikigai: The Japanese Secret to a Long and Happy Life*. Hutchinson London.

Gartenberg, Claudine, Andrea Prat, and George Serafeim. September 2016. *Corporate Purpose and Financial Performance*. Harvard Business School Working Paper No. 17-023.

George, Bill. 2003. *Authentic Leadership: Rediscovering the Secrets to Creating Lasting Value*. Jossey-Bass–Wiley.

Grant, Adam. 2014. *Give and Take: Why Helping Others Drives Our Success*. OrionBooks.

Hedges, Kristi. 2011. *The Power of Presence—Unlock Your Potential to Influence and Engage Others*. Amacom.

Ibarra, Herminia. 2015. *Act Like a Leader, Think Like a Leader*. Harvard Business Review Press.

Ibarra, Herminia. 2003. *Working Identity—Unconventional Strategies for Reinventing Your Career*. Harvard Business School Press.

Locke, Edwin A., and Gary P. Latham. 2017. *New Developments in Goal Setting and Task Performance*. Routledge.

Mackey, John, Steve McIntosh, and Carter Phipps. 2020. *Conscious Leadership*. Portfolio/ Penguin.

Mackey, John, and Raj Sisodia. 2014. *Conscious Capitalism: Liberating the Heroic Spirit of Business*. Harvard Business Review Press.

Malandro, Loretta. 2014. *Speak Up, Show Up, and Stand Out*. McGraw-Hill.

Newport, Cal. 2016. *Deep Work: Rules for Focused Success in a Distracted World*. Grand Central Publishing.

Seligman, Martin E.P. 2004. *Authentic Happiness: Using the New Positive Psychology to Realize Your Potential for Lasting Fulfillment*. Simon & Schuster.

Seligman, Martin E.P. 2011. *Flourish: A Visionary New Understanding of Happiness and Well-Being*. Simon & Schuster.

Seligman, Martin E.P. 1990. *Learned Optimism: How to Change Your Mind and Your Life*. Random House.

Shell, G. Richard. 2012. *Springboard: Launching Your Personal Search for Success*. Penguin.

Sher, Barbara. 1994. *I Could Do Anything If I Only Knew What It Was*. Dell Publishing.

Sinek, Simon, David Mead, and Peter Docker. 2017. *Find Your Why*. Portfolio Penguin.

ABOUT THE AUTHOR

In her 20-plus years in the financial services industry, Dr. Kathrin Anne Meier has held leading positions, including Chief Risk Officer for insurance companies, and she has also been an executive and non-executive board member for top-tier corporations. She regularly shares her broad knowledge about risk management as well as the knowhow she obtained in leadership, employee development, and mentoring over her long career. With her company Corporate Life Mastery, she provides training for leaders and aspiring leaders in the corporate world. Being genuinely interested in people, she knows and understands very well employees' worries and needs, as well as the importance of finding happiness, fun, and joy in corporate work. Her company provides transformative training in core skills such as leadership, thinking, and other people skills to help leaders expand their minds and achieve real-world impact.

She holds a master's degree in mathematics and a PhD in computer science, both from the Swiss Federal Institute of Technology in Zurich, Switzerland, as well as an MBA in Financial Services from the University of St. Gallen, Switzerland.

Lightning Source UK Ltd.
Milton Keynes UK
UKHW010632231222
414374UK00001B/93

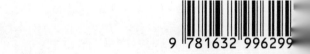